HEALING

HEALING

Selected Lessons from Archangel Gabriel

Channeled by
Reverend Penny Donovan

Edited by Peter Santos

Sacred Garden Fellowship, Inc.
Albany, New York

Published by Sacred Garden Fellowship, Inc.
Albany, NY
www.sacredgardenfellowship.org

ISBN-13: 978-1932746020

Acknowledgements

This book would not have been possible without the support and efforts of many in the Sacred Garden Fellowship (SGF) community including Donald Gilbert, Virgil McIntosh, Peter Santos, and of course Reverend Penny Donovan. In addition, the contributions of many others in the SGF community have been essential to sustaining SGF and promoting its mission, helping bring the organization to a place where it's possible to bring this book into publication. SGF also offers deep loving gratitude to the nonphysical teachers, guides, and angels who have been there every step of the way, challenging us and offering opportunities for both the organization and the community to grow spiritually, and guiding us ever forward on the path to Truth. And finally, many thanks to the reader who has been drawn to these lessons and is now joined on the path of advancing themselves towards awakening the divinity within.

Table of Contents

Preface

In October of 1987, my life changed very drastically one Sunday. I went to church, as I had done for twenty-three years. As I went into my office to get my Bible and get ready to go up on the podium, I felt very light-headed and dizzy and I thought, "Well, I ate dinner early. Maybe I just need some food." The feeling kind of passed as I went out on the podium.

I remember saying to the congregation, "Before I give my talk, we have a meditation." The last thing I remember was the meditation. The next thing I knew I was standing at the lectern with everyone standing up and applauding! I didn't know what had happened. The people were saying, "It was wonderful! A teacher came."

It was during the next few days that the teacher revealed himself to me as being the Archangel Gabriel. He said, "I will teach you things and if you will follow and do them, they will change your life for the better."

That was the beginning of the twelve years during which he channeled through me, teaching truths and providing spiritual guidance. His teachings were simple, loving. I watched the people in my congregation change, evolve, and grow.

He was challenged many times by me and others, and never did he lose his temper. He never was anything but loving and kind, and he never failed to have an answer to any question that was given to him. He was a very powerful, loving force in my life and in the lives of the people who came to hear him over the years.

People have often asked me what it was like to channel Gabriel and how I felt after he left us for good in 1999. For a long time it was difficult to put into words the feelings I had of the channeling and his leaving. I awoke one morning and the words were there and I share them now with you.

Gabriel was an energy, a divine energy, that overtook my consciousness and my body from an indefinable Source. He was not greater than I, but he was more powerful and strong-willed with an intent of absolute love and goodness. He overrode my fears and caused me to be so still that I seemed to disappear. I was aware of him, bound and consumed in the love of him. My surrender was complete and only in retrospect do I realize how totally I trusted him. Once I surrendered, I never entertained the idea of stopping.

When it was over, I felt an emptiness inside, an emptiness that rises to the surface now and then as a great longing for something lost before time began. Yet at other times the mere memory of him brings a comfort beyond words. It will never be again, yet it will never be totally gone. Gabriel left something of himself that will be with me always, beyond earth or heaven;

an addition to the fabric that is my true self, a gift more pure than mind can comprehend. And so it is.

Reverend Penny Donovan

Introduction

Reverend Penny Donovan is a psychic who has been a natural medium since childhood. She studied under Reverend Edith S. Wendling at the John Carlson Memorial Institute in Buffalo, NY where she was ordained in 1960. She obtained her Doctor of Divinity degree from the Fellowships of the Spirit in Buffalo, NY.

In 1964, she founded the Trinity Temple of the Holy Spirit Church in Albany, NY where she served as pastor for thirty years. To devote more time to the teachings of Archangel Gabriel, in November 1994, she retired as pastor of Trinity Temple and founded Springwell Metaphysical Studies. In January 2005, she established a new organization called The Gabriel Fellowship for the preservation, publication, and teaching of Gabriel's lessons. This organization merged with the Sacred Garden Retreats organization, founded by Donald Gilbert, LCSW, in November 2009 to become the Sacred Garden Fellowship (SGF).

SGF makes available audios, books, and booklets of Archangel Gabriel and Rev. Penny's and Don Gilbert's seminars and lectures. The organization also conducts regular meetings to support those who seek spiritual guidance and continued expansion of their knowledge and understanding of spiritual truths. It is SGF's desire that, in all these lessons, the reader finds truths that resonate within and deeply touch their life.

Archangel Gabriel taught for twelve years from October 1987 to December 1999 at evening lectures and all-day seminars, usually one or two times a month but sometimes more often. When he identified himself to Rev. Penny, there was a concern that listeners might become attached to the excitement and drama around the channeling of an archangel and follow or idolize Gabriel or Rev. Penny herself. So, in order to keep the focus on the lessons, Gabriel decided to call himself Lucas in the early lectures.

His talks were primarily given in Albany, New York where Rev. Penny lived. However, she did travel to other locations to provide opportunities for Gabriel to teach different audiences. Most of his seminars and lectures were audio taped, resulting in over 250 recorded sessions.

Over the years, Gabriel's teachings covered a wide spectrum of spiritual truths ranging from the nature of God and who we are as Spirit to our current level of evolvement and spiritual understanding in this physical dimension. He explained how and why we are here on earth, our purpose for being here, and what we must do to return home to our remembrance of our Spirit within.

He covered many topics such as our levels of consciousness, reincarnation, energy, our egos, the power of our thoughts, negative and positive thinking, unconditional love, forgiveness, and the purpose of the experiences we go through in our lives. His central theme was always for us to live our truth through unconditional love, compassion, and forgiveness, and with the knowing that we are truly the Children of God.

As he said he would, Gabriel taught his final lesson in December 1999. Since then, Rev. Penny has continued to present spiritual truths through her writings, classes, and in conjunction with Donald Gilbert, conduct spiritual retreats where she continues to teach and channel master teachers, including Yeshua (the Master Jesus).

Rev. Penny's love of God, her teaching and channeling talents, her ability to incorporate lessons in truth gleaned and developed from a lifetime of spiritual learning and growth, and her desire to help others find their spiritual path and highest good are a gift to us and our world.

After channeling through Rev. Penny for twelve years, Gabriel made it clear that he would not be returning to the earth plane for another two thousand years. However, in May 2015, he made a surprise visit during an SGF weekend retreat that was on the topic of how his material would be taught to others. SGF had put together a first level curriculum of Gabriel's materials—including a video, an introductory book of selected sessions, and a syllabus for a nine-week course—and Gabriel blessed us with his presence to clarify how his wonderful teachings are to be presented.

From his words at that retreat:

The teachings that I have given on the earth plane through this beloved woman are not to be changed in any way. They are to be taught verbatim as it was given. There shall be no interpretation of it, no addition of, "This is important. You don't have to pay attention to that." You are to teach it *word for word*.

If you feel it necessary to give an example to whomever you are teaching, you will say, "These are not Gabriel's words. These are my words. I found a benefit by thinking what he said in this way." But you are not to change one word of what I gave. The reason being... What I gave is pure Truth, absolute pure Truth from the highest there is. It is given to the earth plane in its Truth. It loses value when it is interpreted, when it is dissected, and all this sort of thing.

And later...

Don't interpret what you are transcribing. Transcribe it word for word, even if the language is incorrect.

This volume of unedited transcripts by Archangel Gabriel contains his words as they were spoken. As such, copyediting to accepted standards such as the *Chicago Manual of Style* was not a priority. Instead, as directed, the text is word for word from the audio recordings, including seeming inconsistencies in grammar.

In addition, care was taken to reflect Gabriel's manner of speaking and emphasis on particular words or phrases. His frequent pauses and recurrent use of "now," "and," and "but" at the beginning of sentences were also retained.

Most of the time, Gabriel's voice comes through the recordings quite strongly and clearly (as he is a powerful speaker) but there are occasional inaudible words or phrases when his voice was softer and/or when the recording did not pick up the sound well. Even though sometimes the inaudible word or phrase seems obvious, it is indicated in the text as "[inaudible]" so the reader can make his or her own decision as to the meaning.

While in Rev. Penny's physical form, Gabriel sometimes jokes around with the group he is teaching. He also occasionally speaks or consults with his playful angel helper, known as Tinkerbell, who has a better understanding of earthly matters than he does and who delights in joking and finding joy in even the smallest of things. These digressions from the lessons are typically included to show his grand and wondrous personality.

This book contains selected teachings on healing from Gabriel's twelve years of lessons. Although it is not a complete compilation of all that he shared on the topic, it covers the major concepts about healing and what it means to be a healer.

It is Sacred Garden Fellowship's hope that the reader truly *feels* the teachings contained in this volume and aspires to practice and *live* the lessons as given. This is the first point in SGF's mission; "To encourage all to become aware of and live from their God-Self."

May you be blessed on your journey.

HEALING

Selected Lessons from
Archangel Gabriel

Healing Enlightenment
November 5 & 12, 1988

Archangel Gabriel: [known as Lucas at the time]
Ah, beloved of God, we have congregated! Indeed. Welcome to all of you. Why have we come this day? Is it not to learn? Indeed. [Speaking to the roses] Ah, beauteous entities, welcome to thee. Blessed art thou. Your presence adds much, indeed. Thank you. Lemon water. Ah.

[Caution had been expressed to Gabriel concerning accidentally stepping off the platform.] Fear not. If I step off, she will float...or at least I will. (Laughter)

When you think of healing, what think you? Think you there be an absence of that which is called disease? Or think you that there be a replacement with good health of that which is termed ill health? Which think you that it be, for they are not the same? Absence of disease.

Now, I tell you a wondrous truth... All illness, disease—whether it be of the physical body, of the mind, of your emotional body—is an illusion. "Ah," you say, "that is because you have never had a toothache." Indeed, I have not. (Laughter) An illusion

3

is that which *appears* to be a truth but has no basis of fact.

Now, in your perception, you have created that which you believe to be a truth. This can take any form and often does. You can believe that you are very poor and it will manifest. You can believe you are wondrous indeed—as I be, as you all be, for we are as one—and that will manifest also.

Now, everyone thinks that they are a victim of their physical beings. Someone would say, "Ah, I would go off to rejoice and have revelry excepting that my head pains me greatly, therefore I am subject to it. It tells me I must rest so therefore I do." Now, if you think these things, who be the boss? You or the physical house you occupy? Ah, indeed.

Now, when there is healing—and you listen to this closely please—when there is healing, it is of the *mind*, for the body will give you *exactly* what your *mind dictates*. So, whether it be the laying on of hands, the taking in of substance, whatever it be that you do *to your* body, has no bearing until you do *with* your body through your mind.

Know you what swearing be? Cursing? Know you that that was the beginning of physical illness? Ah, you did not know that did you? You thought it was germs. (Laughter)

In your perfect state—and you all are perfect, every one of you—you are a direct power. You are...the closest that you have in your words is electricity. That is the closest word that I can bring to you in your words that will explain what you are. You are without form. You are without any imperfection. You have

4

brought this down into form. You have created what you *appear* to be. You have the power—and you do it...you say, "Ah, not me," but you do it—to create anything that you want. *Anything*. There are no exceptions.

Now, when first you began to create wondrous things, it was beautiful. Everything you created was a joy—flowers, creatures, trees whatever. Then there entered in the idea that *you* and *God* were no longer together. There came a bringing down into error your concept of yourself and of others.

You began to perceive that something was good and something else was not good, and in order to compensate for that which was not good, you had to create something else that was better. And what entered in here was competition, a state of competition. Know you what that be? Indeed. You must run faster than your neighbor or have a bigger mode of transportation or bigger picture box, better figure among the ladies, be taller among the gentlemen, or whatever. In your competition, you drew away from your knowingness of love because when you stopped off...fantasize that you could stop loving...actually you cannot, you know. You slide love down the scale to what you perceive to be hate but it still is a powerful emotion and therein came the beginning of illness. You withdrew, in your perception, love and in the withdrawing of it, you choked off a life force. Follow you what I say so far? Indeed. You are a bright and wondrous bunch, are you not? (Laughter)

Now there came your perception that you had no power, that what you thought and what you said mattered not, but there were those among you who knew, who *knew* that there is a *power* in the spoken word and they used it to manipulate, to control, to hold from you your knowingness. That took the form of cursing or swearing, whatever you want to call it, and in the use of those words there came condemnation.

Know you how it be...we have taught you in your books you read, you speak to flowers, to plants, and you bring forth their beauty? They know that you love them. Same with little creatures, same with children, new babes. Know you how you go to a little young one. You pick it up and you hold it and you say, "I love you grandly." Know you how it smiles and gurgles and comes forth with its joy? Now, what happens if you pick up this little babe and instead of saying that you love it, if you curse it? What think you that it do? Think you that it gurgle and laugh at you? No.

In the condemning, through *your* words, of each other... Now, when I speak of each other and all of you, I do not refer to *you* only. I do not single you out and say, "Ah, you." I talk about humankind, all of those who have dwelt upon the earth plane from whenever. When you began to curse one another, you were taking that which was pure and holy—the goodness of you, the God of you—and you used your power for ill.

The priests and the scribes of old remembered their Source and this is the power they used over the masses, for the masses were ignorant. They had forgotten where they came from. They had forgotten that they were created perfect, that their spoken word had great and wondrous power, and so they used it not and they lived in fear.

Now, along comes priest and scribe—of whatever religion. I do not single anyone out. They are all guilty or not as you choose to look—and they knew the power of the spoken word and so they held it over the heads, as it were, of the masses and they said, "If you do not do thus-and-so, you shall be cursed unto hell." And they trembled in fear.

Know you what hell be? Know you where the word came from? The word "hell" means to be put in a little, narrow, shallow grave. Know you why that struck such terror in the hearts of those who heard it? Because there were great beasts roaming about that used to feed on the carcasses of those who had passed away and it was considered a terrible thing to be placed into a little, shallow grave, for at that time, they buried in tombs. Only those who were cursed were put in little graves. So, every time you say to your fellow people, "You go to hell..." Ah, you did not know I could swear, did you? (Laughter) I have been about, I have listened to you, and I have learned much. (Laughter) Indeed I have been to...where was it I went to, Yale?

Participant: Yale.

Gabriel: And I learned about all the things young men do when they are turned loose. (Laughter) Oh, interesting indeed. Among the things they do is to swear.

In the cursing, there came about the *awareness* in *your* consciousness that there could be an ill fate, that there could come less than that which was good, less than that which was perfect. And as you *accepted that awareness*, you brought it into its fullness and you developed in your physical bodies dis-ease, pain, lack of pleasure, lack of the sense of well-being.

Know you what happens now, today, when you try to do two opposite things as some of you here do? Some of you here do healings, which is wondrous! While you are doing the healings, you are pouring in wondrous energy but then you go out and curse at your modes of transportation that congregate in great long lines to get somewhere all at the same time. (Laughter) Do you not?

Now, see you what I mean about the swearing and the healing? On the on hand, you are calling the power of God, which is perfection. You are bringing it forth. And on the other hand you are cursing. Now which is it going to be? Which are you going to bring to its fullness? That which has the most *emotion*.

Now, when you do your healings, is there a great surge of love for the entity that you are touching? Is there as much power there through what you are *feeling* as there is when you are cursing your fellow creatures? What think you? Anger is a potent force, is it not?

Now, you say, "But they make me angry. I get very frustrated." I know, I ride with Beloved Woman! (Laughter) She gets very angry. She'll say, "Look at that! Does he not know I must be somewhere on time?" No, he does not, nor does he care. (Laughter)

But every one of you does the same thing, perhaps not with modes of transportation, perhaps with fellow creatures in your work, where you work, wherever. All of you here have used cursing, have you not? Ah, indeed. I have been among you.

Now, I tell you a truth... You cannot do both. If you be healers, and you all here are, then you must learn to draw *away from* the vibration—and it is a very low vibration, a very earthy one—of cursing. 'Tis not easy. Anything becomes a habit.

Know you what happens when you say, "God damn it," to someone? Think of the words you use. God, the same God that you call upon when you say Lord God of my being? Indeed. Now, what are you asking this power to do? To *damn* something. Know you what that means? I have found out you use this word in two ways: to curse and to hold back water. Indeed, I tell you you are not holding back water. (Laughter) You are asking that that which is sacred and holy—that which *sustains life, gives* life, *is* life— *take* life, *take* love and *destroy* it. You are asking it to do that which it is *not capable of* and you are asking it to be done with great emotion and power. So, what is happening inside of you when you do this? What think you is going on in the metabolism of your being when you ask the God that is life to destroy?

Think you it will give you flush cheeks, good health, strong bodies? You are taking the *life* that is in you, which is your *power*, and you are *twisting* it and you are causing it to make, to create, that which is *foul* and that which is foul is going to manifest where? *In* you.

Now you say, "But I know of those who are very ill who have never spoken an ill word." But you do not know what they think, for I tell you a truth... There is no illness that is not created by ill thought. I care not how it manifests, whether it be a toothache or a hanging up nail...hanging down nail? (Laughter) Hanging nail? Just hanging? Oh, indeed. Whatever, be it serious or temporary, it matters not. It comes from an ill thinking.

Now, this illness, this dis-ease, it is as much an illusion as your physical beings are. Now, you say, "My physical being is not an illusion! Behold, I am in it every day." But I tell you a truth... The truth of you, that which is real of you, is Spirit and anything else is a heavier and heavier and heavier vibration until you have created layer upon layer upon layer of covering around your Spirit, and the coverings that you have created are the illusions.

Know you what inter-dimensional travel be? Know you how you can use your mind to be somewhere your physical body is not? You do it, all of you. I have watched you daydream and fantasize. Some of you go back into the past. Others of you go into the future. Some of you just go next door. But you travel with your thoughts, always. Because there is inter-dimensional livingness, the more solid the form appears, the more of an illusion that it be. Can you understand that? No? Ah.

If you took light, which all of you are, and you slowed its vibration, it would take form of some kind. It would have to. In the taking of the form, it would be not the electricity that you see...think you this...what you call those? Light bulbs. Think you that they be electricity? They are the outer covering that gives manifestation to that which would be invisible to your

10

sight without them. Know you what I say? Ah, so it 'tis with you. The Spirit of you has no form. It doesn't need one. But you choose to take a form in order that you might be visible.

Now, the center of you, this which is invisible, has no illness. The bodies that you create are not meant to have illness. Know that your bodies are wondrous works. They are walking miracles. Know you this? Do you ever say to your heart, "Keep beating"? Do you ever say to your lungs, "Breathe"? Do you ever order the blood to flow through your body to take oxygen to your brain? Do you ever tell your livers to take out all the bile and all of the awful things that you have placed within your body? Do you ever ask your bowels to empty? Indeed not. You go about your business. They do all these things by themselves, do they not?

So, they would manifest in *perfect health* if you *let* them. If you do not interfere with your physical bodies and their functioning, they are created to function in *perfect order*. But they are also created to follow *exactly* what the *mind* tells them and it is your *mind* that you must work with.

When someone needs healing, all of you here work with the physical body. But I tell you a truth... Unless the mind of your...is the word patient? Is that not what makes you want to wait a bit? Two patients as there are two dams! Ah, indeed I have it! (Laughter)

Now, when you work upon the physical being of your patient, you are only working with the *effect*, not the cause. Know you what I say? "Ah," but you say, " 'tis the effect that hurts!" Indeed! But unless the cause is changed, all of the healing in the world of the effect is not going to bring the person into perfect health, for if they do not manifest one ailment, they shall manifest another, so you must work with the *mind*.

Now, you say, "Ah, but the body I can touch. How touch I their mind?" You can only change your own mind. You cannot change another but you can give them tools to work with. And this is what healing is all about.

Now, I have been here and I have watched you with the laying-on of hands, working with crystals, working with all wondrous things. Pyramids, some of you here use pyramids. All of these have power, the power that you give them, the power that you bring forth from them, that which you call out of them in your belief. And they all work. But to truly heal, which is what you all want, you have to go *past* the outer and to the center, to the *cause* of it.

Your physicians, they give you medication that eases your suffering. They have nothing to give you to heal your body. Every medication brings results of some kind but none of them heals. Know you what heals? The mind of the patient! If a patient decides, "Behold, I am going to pass away," nothing the physicians can do will save them. If the patient decides, "Behold, I shall get well," nothing the physicians can do will hinder it. And some of them try, you know. Not on purpose. It is in your *mind*, and this is the point that you must work from.

Some of you here can lay your hand upon a fellow being and take away a headache. Some of you here can wither away tumors. Some of you here can make pain go away in any part of the body you touch. Know you

12

how you do that? I know how you *think* you do it, but know you how you do it? Because the God in you has touched the God in your patient and has awakened in that patient the realization that all of their illness is an illusion. It is a product of their thinking, of their words, and it has no power over them, no power.

Now you say, "But I do not know how I do this." But the God of you knows. Know you what the Holy Spirit be? It is the bridge between the God of you and the lord of you. The lord of you is that which creates your perception, your illusion. The God of you is that which knows the truth of you. The Holy Spirit is aware of the God of you and is also aware of where the lord of you be.

Now, in that Holy Spirit, which is in everyone, there is a knowingness of perfect health, perfect state of well-being, perfect manifestation of any joy that you wish, and it is that which brings the lord of you up into that knowingness and you are healed.

Would you like to be able to lay your hands upon anyone and heal them of anything? You can. There is no illness, no illness that cannot be healed. Now, you say, "But I have sent healing to so-and-so and so-and-so and they get..." Oh, there be one who sent healings and the person died and they thought the healing had failed. No, they had chosen to withdraw.

Now...first I have a little lemon water. Beloved Woman's throat grows dry. In a little bit, we shall break-up? Take a break. (Laughter) Ah, indeed. Well, I have the right concept. Yes, indeed.

It is not necessary to *labor* to give healing. Healing is a *natural* thing. It is that which is your right to be perfectly healthy. It is not something you have to work at. Now, what happens, do you think, when you give healings and the patient does not get well? Oh, they do not pass away. They just stay the same. What think you is going on? Think you that you have failed? Think you that you have failed?

Participant: No, you haven't failed. They have failed to receive.

Gabriel: Ah, indeed. Now, they have received your healing. They have not taken it *within*. They have not allowed it to be a part of them. They have *not accepted* it. Do you think that they never shall? Perhaps, but the moment that they do, behold, what happens? They are healed!

You should give each patient one healing only. No one needs more than that, for if you feel that the person needs more, then you are failing to realize your Source. You are failing to see that the perfection in them and the perfection in you has *met* and behold, wondrous things have taken place.

Now, you say, "But people come for healings for this and healings for that and healings for something else." If they receive a healing for...oh, beloved woman, give me an ailment...a hang nail. That is an illness? (Laughter)

Participant: Pain in the neck.

Gabriel: That is a person, no? (Laughter) Pain, pain in the neck is here? [Points to neck] Yes. If they come to you for a pain in the neck—or any other part of the anatomy for that matter. Other people have pains elsewhere, do they not? Indeed—and you give them a healing and the pain is dispelled, and the next day they

14

come back and they say, "Behold, my appendage aches." Now, what do you think has happened? Think you that the healing you have given them has worked only here [neck] and has not touched the rest of them? No. Healing is for *all* of them. The whole person is touched and healed. Now, if they manifest a pain in the appendage, what have *they* done? Have they not transferred their error thoughts from one part of their anatomy to another? Have they not said, "Oh, behold the pain is gone. I must manifest another," and do it?

"Ah," you say, "No one wants to be sick." But they do. Think you that there be no benefits in being ill? Ah, your perceptions, your error thinking would have you know that there is. If you are ill, someone somewhere is going to feel sorry for you, are they not? Is this not a grand and wondrous way to get attention if you are alone and lonely or feel unloved? Is it not also a great and wondrous way to make others feel guilty? Is it not a good way to manipulate someone else? Think about it. Who know you that is ill that does not use it in some way to hold onto another? Think about it. Beloved woman in the back has many wondrous patients, have you not? Can you not see what I am saying in your patients? Ah, indeed.

Now, this applies to you, too. If you wake up in the morn and your body tells you that you are aching, who is going to take care of you? Some of you say, "Ah, there be no one." But there be someone somewhere who would say, "Oh, poor thing. Better you have little sympathy. Stay home, have a cup of tea. I will do your errands. I will take care of your offspring or whatever. I will do your job."

What about older parents who have grown children who live a distance away? Is this not a wondrous way to get everyone congregated about the deathbed, so to say? Ah. Then miraculously the parent recovers after everyone has journeyed far to see them. Have you not known this to happen? Most of all, is it not a wondrous way to rest when you feel guilty about resting if you are *not* ill?

How many of you here are comfortable with staying in your beds in the morning until the hour grows late? You think, "Oh, I *should* be up," do you not? But if a part of your anatomy is in dis-ease, ache, or pain somewhere, is it not a grand and wondrous excuse to stay there and not have anyone think, "Ah, they be lazy bones"? (Laughter) Is it not? Ah. You see, it is this kind of thinking that brings forth from your inner self the idea of aches and pains and dis-ease. It is your clogging up of your system of flow through your cursing that block the truth of you from manifesting in perfect health.

In the healing of the physical body, you must first begin with your own. If you would heal another, you must have a clear, concise knowingness of perfect health. Now, this is not to say everyone here should stop doing their healing, but you must work on your own self first.

Now, your physical bodies are the temple of the living God and they are precious. They are wondrous. They are to be loved and to be cherished. When you think of them...everyone here is guilty of this, for I have been among you. Is it not wondrous to know you are being spied upon? (Laughter)

Some of you here complain because you are too short. Beloved Woman is guilty of this. Some of you are too tall, some of you are too fat, some too thin, some too old, some too young, some too dark, some too light, some too this, some too that. There is not one entity in this room who has not a complaint against this physical body.

Some of you here wish you looked like another entity. Some of you here wish that you could change *everything* about yourself. Ah, I tell you what... Your physical bodies, whatever they are—tall, short, fat, thin, old, young, whatever—are exactly what you created them to be. And because you created them to be thus, you should love them, cherish them, see their beauty, know them as miraculous, wondrous, and perfect in every way.

If you feel you want to change your appearance...and that's all that it is, you know. You wish to change your appearance so that the world would look upon you and say, "Ah, how beauteous." But I tell you, every *one* of you here is beauteous, everyone. If you would change your appearance, you begin by changing your *concept* of your appearance, for no one else ever sees you the way *you* see you, ever.

You can rise in the morning, go before your reflective glasses and say, "Oh, I look terrible today." And you go forth into the world and someone will say, "Oh, how becoming you are this day," and you say, "Oh no, I look terrible." Now, what think you that you be doing to your physical beings when you do this? Think you that your body is going to give you the becomingness another sees? Or is it going to give you the terribleness that you behold? Who is capable of programming your body? Your neighbor or you? Yourself.

Now, while you dwell upon the earth plane, you must dwell in the physical body, otherwise you are not seen by your fellow creatures. Oh, sometimes that is not so bad either, is it? (Laughter) But the bodies that you occupy are yours. There are a few around who loan them out, like Beloved Woman loans me hers, but I always give it back. 'Tis too cumbersome. (Laughter) Oh, tell her not I said that. She shall go on a grand and wondrous diet. (Laughter)

The thing is this, that you occupy your body. You are *not* your body but you occupy it, and while you occupy it, it serves your purpose, does it not? Does it not take you about to manifest what you need? It is your ability to function on the earth and you must cherish it and love it and see it for what it is, a perfectly functioning form that you have created and you are dwelling in.

Now, when the time comes that you no longer need it, you will lay it aside, but do so lovingly. Do not ravish it with dis-ease. You do not need to die with something, as they say. When you finish your incarnation here and you wish to leave, if you do not desire to take your body with you, then lay it lovingly aside, bless it unto the earth or unto the air, however you choose, but do not curse it with illness.

There are those who do terrible things to their physical bodies. They pour into them chemicals, smoke, all kinds of awful things. They rob them of their proper diets. They refuse to allow them the proper rest. Know you why your physical bodies need sleep? You do not sleep, your bodies do. Know you why this be? Because the Spirit of you needs to lay aside the cumbersomeness, the heaviness—and this is true no matter how light you be—and go unto the Father again and let the body rest. Then in the morn, you come back and take up residency again. Your body is rested and you have grown some in your knowingness and you go about your daily tasks. Did you know that you did this? Is it not wondrous? You think you have to stay upon the earth plane from your birth until the end of your time? Oh, no. You leave it every...how many hours you have? Twenty hours? Twenty-four hours. Once in every twenty-four hours you vacate and you go elsewhere and you take up busyness up there while your body slumbers, for the brain is not able to keep up with the mind.

Your nervous system needs a rest. You go into a state of mild hibernation while you sleep. Your heart rate slows, your breathing slows, everything comes down, down, down. And while it is resting, you are free! You go about and you do wondrous things. You go to school, some of you. Some of you go and heal. Beloved entity here, he goes about to hospitals at night. Did you know this?

A lot of you do great and wondrous things. You, beloved woman, you go among the creatures. You do all kinds of interesting things. Some of you go with little entities that are newly arrived in spirit and help them to adjust. Some of you travel out into the universes and learn of new and wondrous ways of life. Some of you go to a very peaceful place and drink in the beauty of it. You do this many times. Sometimes I pass you when you are going, with a tip of the hat and a, "How do you do?" and away you go. (Laughter)

Some of you visit those who have passed away. But whatever you choose, your physical body is in a state of suspended animation in which it is refurbished, it takes on new energies, new strength. Some of you bring back to it a *new* energy, a lighter one, so that... Have you not ever woke in the morn and thought, "Oh, what a glorious day!" and felt full of energy and vitality? Have you not done this? That is because your journey has taken you to new awarenesses and you bring back with you that new awareness and you put it into the cells of your brain and you *know more.*

How think you that you can go to slumber at night with a great problem upon your mind and awake in the morning and think "Oh, behold, I know what I shall do. I shall do thus-and-so." How think you that you find your answer? In your pillow case? (Laughter) No, indeed. The Spirit of you travels to where you can *know.*

Now you say, "What...how has this to do with healing?" Everything. Your body requires food. Certain kinds of food are good for you, certain other kinds are harmful. Your body requires rest. You have to let your brain, all of your body, rest. If you deprive it of good food, if you deprive it of rest, if you cause it to take unto itself things that are not natural to it, then you are setting it *off.* It doesn't know what you want from it and it will be out of balance, and when it becomes out of balance, the hormones do not work correctly.

Know you what **hormones** do? They give you balance. Know you why they are called hormones? It is taken from the Latin word homines, to be in harmony with. If you do not *allow* your physical body these things, it is not going to bear you well, is it? It will break down, as it were, before you are finished with it. Then you have to go and get it repaired. You do not have to do this.

The cells of your body replenish themselves again and again and again. Know you that you become new every seven years of your earthly life? Know you this? Know that you can take on to yourselves a youthfulness and a vitality and a strength that *never* need to be dissipated?

You have taken into your consciousness the idea of old age and discrepancy...decrepancy? Discrepancy means to tell a falsehood, is this not so? So, it would be decrepitcy? Ah, see, I am learning! Indeed.

You have taken these ideas unto yourselves and you think you must play them out, as it were, in your physical bodies. You think, "Oh, behold, I am so many years of earthly life. Oh, therefore I must start to be lame or I must start to be this or my eyes begin to fail or something." None of this is true. You can be in *perfect* health with *all* faculties intact up unto the time you lay aside your physical body if this is what you want, but it is *your* decision.

You do not have to grow old. That is an illusion. That is something you expect because you see others doing it. Have you not met some people who are eternally youthful? You are not sure exactly how many earthly years old they are, are you? And when you find out, you are amazed. It is because they have tuned into the *ongoingness* of life. They realize the physical body is a treasure. It is to be loved and revered and thought well of. It is *not* you, but it is what *you* use and you must take good care of it.

Now, I digress a moment. When I said to you that you give but *one* healing, this is a truth, for if you give more than one healing to a single entity, you are cancelling out the truth of their being in perfect health. Know you what I mean? If you took a container [picks up a glass of water]...I shall be careful not to spill. If you take a container and you fill it full, you say to yourself, "Ah behold, it is full. It will hold no more." Would you then come back a moment later and say, "I shall fill it again," even though it be full? No, you would not, would you? You would behold and say, "It is still full." So it is when you give a healing. You are *filling*, you are filling the *wholeness* of that person with *God-life* and that does not dissipate. It does not become lesser. Therefore, if you come back a moment later or a year later or whenever, you do not need to do it again. Know you what I say?

It matters not what outer form you use for healing. Some of you prefer crystals, some of you prefer pyramids, some of you prefer the laying-on of hands, whatever. That is only the outward manifestation of your inward desire to bring well-being to another, so it matters not what form. Some of you will say, "Oh, this way is better than that way." There is no better. It is all the same Source, is it not?

It is God manifesting, matter it not whether it be this way or that way. What matters is that you be the channel through which this flows.

Now, I go back again to the cursing. You cannot get clear water from a rusty pipe, and every time you condemn someone or yourself, you are adding rust and corrosion to the channel that you are. Know you this? Now, is everyone going to stop cursing?

All: Yes.

Gabriel: Indeed. 'Till next time. It is a truth, beloveds. If you would speak the word of God, then do not let curse words cross your lips. Do not condemn your physical bodies by damning parts of it or thinking parts of it are dirty or foul. There is nothing foul about your body, nothing. There is no part of your anatomy that is any more precious than any the rest of it. And to call another a name, which would bring down the physical form, is a terrible thing that *you* do to *yourselves*, not to the other. Every time you think that any portion of you or another is foul in any form, you are lessening yourself, not the other.

You have phrases that you use. I shall not speak them here for Beloved Woman would be...oh, I shudder to think of what she would say to me. I do not need to name them; you know them. Phrases that you use that would belittle and curse some part of your anatomy or another. Some acts that you do that are perfectly natural, you befoul by making them *less* in your cursing. Know you what I mean?

You take a beauteous act of love—of caring, caressing, holding, loving, sharing, being together—between a man and a woman and you befoul it by making it seem to be a dirty thing, and you use that as an expression of cursing. You even use hand gestures that represent this in a most foul manner. Oh, I have been among you. I have watched you. Why take you this beautiful act—it's holy and sacred—and make it into something that is befouled when it is not?

The sexual act between people who love one another is a most wondrous thing. It is the outer expression of a joining together of two halves that make a whole. It is the outer expression of the soul of you desiring to be At-one-ment with the Father. It should not be brought into the gutter. It should be treasured, respected, and thought of as a most wondrous expression of love.

But if you use it in a cursing way, if you declare unto another to go by themselves to do this deed alone, and you use that as matter of cursing, know you what you are doing to your sexual organs when you do this? You are inviting all kinds of terrible things unto them. I believe you have a name for it called cancer. Blockages of various and sundry things, ways of befouling it so they do not function.

What about the waste the body casts off after you have had a meal? Know you how you use this in a derogatory sense? If you dropped something or something goes amiss for you, there is a word you have that you use. You say, "Oh, ----." (Laughter) Do you not? It's a natural functioning of the body. If it did not occur, you would be in grand trouble, would you not? So, why curse you? Why think you that it be not good?

You even take things of nature and incorporate them into your cursing. There is a term you use...bull.

Have you not? 'Tis a favorite of Beloved Woman's (laughter), only she uses the initials...changes it not! She says, "Oh, BS!" (Laughter) Now, I tell you something... That is a natural functioning of a creature's body, is it not? It is not foul, it doesn't even smell bad. Your perceptions would have you believe that the very things of nature, the outworkings of your physical being, are wrong and they are not. It is in *your perception* that they be foul and *only* in *your* perception.

Now, every time you use these expressions... You say, "What has this to do with healing?" Everything, everything, for to be a healer you must have *respect* and *love* for your fellow creatures, must you not? Could you ask the God of them to manifest in perfect health if you do not love them? What care you if you do not love them whether they be well or ill? What care you about your own physical body if you *damn it* because it is not what you think it should be? It is too fat or too small or too tall or too something else or you have not a beauteous face? Why condemn you your own creations for what they are *not* when *you* made them and *invited to* them *through* this condemnation the illnesses that your body will manifest, for it is damned in your sight? And it will give you a damned expression if that's what you expect of it. Understand you my words? Have you learned this day?

When you want to heal, you must first love. You must first put aside your ego.

Know you that there be three reasons why people want to be healers? And some of you here will be offended at this. I do not wish to offend. I wish to bring you truth. The first is because you desire, through love, to see all of your fellow creatures in perfect health because you care about them.

The second is because you fear that you will lose some beloved one in death. You desire greatly for that person to be well, for what will become of *you* if they are not? What will become of you if they make a transition? You should be abandoned, you should be left alone, you should be bereft of their presence.

The third is because you are egotistical and you want others to say, "Ah behold, so-and-so is a grand and wondrous healer!"

Only the first reason I gave you is valid to be a healer. If you do not do it with love, do not do it, for all of the other reasons will produce results exactly opposite the reason you are doing it. If you do it out of fear, you will not produce healing. You will produce more fear, for that is the emotion that is feeding your action. If you do it out of ego, your ego will get great and your patient will wither.

Whatever your *purpose* is what you will manifest. That is why I say to you, "Love is the only reason to be a healer." Desiring to see your fellow human beings in perfect health, manifesting the God within them in joy, in love, in ability to *be* all that they are meant to be because there are no limitations. How we are doing?

Participant: Wonderful.

Gabriel: Ah, she is my grandest fan. (Laughter) I shall invite questions from...what is it they say...from the floor. I don't think the floor has anything to say. (Laughter)

Participant: What you would have us do then...is if we have a healing list, throw it out?

Gabriel: Oh, no. No, no.

Participant: Use it once?

Gabriel: Use it once. Beloved entity, you have *wondrous* healing powers. You know this. When you send a healing to another, you have done *all* that you can do that *one* time because the God of them and the God of you does not need to be continuously reminded. It is called forth to manifest in perfect health and it will do so.

Participant: Thank you.

Gabriel: Is it not a relief that you do not have your long scroll? (Laughter)

Participant: It's hard to remember all those names.

Gabriel: Ah, indeed.

Participant: I was in France and I met some healers there and one of the healers explained to me a phenomena that happened to him on a piece of meat. He put his hands over that piece of meat for a few days and after a few years, he still had that piece of meat. I would like to know the phenomena that happened to that?

Gabriel: It is still living, beloved woman. The flesh is a living thing. Even if you take a piece of it, if you recognize the life that is within it and you continually call forth that life, it will continue to remain. Know you how? Because it is the energy that is poured into it. You can do this with a flower. Beloved Woman has flowers for sometimes almost two months that are cut because she loves them and talks to them. You can do this with anything. But I tell you a truth, beloved woman... Flesh belongs unto the species that it forms. Know you what I say? And when you deprive a creature of its life that you might have its flesh, if you *must* do that, do it with love. Know you what I say? Now, do you wish to do that same thing as this man you speak of?

Participant: Ah, not really. No, I don't think I need to do it.

Gabriel: You do not, no. You have wondrous healing.

Participant: Thank you very much.

Gabriel: She looks behind the chair, this one. (Laughter)

Participant: A couple of questions: The one on follow-up, you said that for healings, you only have to give it once, and this is for absent healings because in classes we send healings to individuals in our classes on Tuesday night and sometimes we send the same healings to the same person every week.

Gabriel: But you do not need to, beloved woman.

Participant: Even if it is absent healing?

Gabriel: Even absent healings. You are calling forth the God of them to manifest in its perfection and as the mind of the patient accepts that, so shall it be.

Participant: Does the same hold true for Mother Earth?

Gabriel: Indeed. Bless her, for she needs it.

Participant: The second question is back to the swearing words that we sometimes use. Sometimes we do say them with a lot of...energy.

Gabriel: Indeed.

Participant: Yes, and sometimes we say them as a joke, as to be kind of humorous in a situation.

Gabriel: It is the intent but remember, beloved woman, any word that conjures up foulness in your mind should be discarded, whether it be for humor or for whatever, for there is no foulness excepting in the perceptions of humankind. You do not wish to perpetuate foulness?

Participant: No.

Gabriel: Indeed.

Participant: I have, but no. (Laughter)

Gabriel: Oh, all be guilty!

Participant: If someone who you have given a healing to comes back again another time and asks for a healing, what should you say to them without them becoming offended.

Gabriel: Oh, they should not be offended if you explain to them that the God within them is eternal and as you call it forth in the knowingness of their perfect health, that is all that is necessary, for God is not limited. If it makes them feel better, take their hands and have a prayer with them. Pray that their mind is able to accept, to comprehend, and to take into their awareness the idea and truth of perfect health.

Participant: Thank you.

Gabriel: Know you how creatures be healed so quickly? For they have no doubt. It does not enter a creature's mind when you send it healing that the healing will not work. They believe it to be a truth, for indeed it is. They sense the energy, the well-beingness wells up within them. It does not enter their mind to doubt it. It simply is and so it should be with all.

Participant: Yes, they are easy to heal.

Gabriel: Indeed. Your little creature is doing well? Ah, indeed. Ah, beloved woman, how be you? You be short?

Participant: Yes, yes. One of the special people...short. I'm really bothered by the one healing type of thing because what I'm hearing is it negates all that was done before and...a couple of things: one, out of my caring and love for the person, I want do something for them.

Gabriel: Ah, but you have. When you give a healing with love and caring, you have done it. I said to beloved entity, you have done all you can do. To repeat it is not necessary. It does no *more* good to give two then to give one.

Participant: Does it take away? I mean does it take away from the previous one?

Gabriel: It takes away only in as much as it is in *your* mind that one is not enough and in that respect, you are limiting the one. Know you what I say?

Participant: Okay. It just sounds like if a person were to come to me and say, "I want another healing," and I then go and tell this person, "You don't *need* another one," it's almost saying something like...I'm trying to talk that person out of, "You don't need a healing." Does that make sense?

Gabriel: If they perceive they need a healing, do as I said to beloved woman. Take their hand and say, "Let me join with you in prayer," and ask that their understanding be opened to accept that which is already theirs, for you have given it.

Participant: So we are conserving energy. (Laughter)

Gabriel: Oh, no. The energy is not to be depleted in healing, but what I tell you is that *one* healing is all there is, whether you ask for it once or a hundred times, it is still the *one healing*.

Participant: So we can heal the whole world once is what you're saying. Is that so?

Gabriel: Of course, if the whole world would accept it. There are those right here in this room now, if I were to lay my hand upon them, I would heal them, but only if they accepted it to be so. There are those here I could lay my hand upon, they would heal. I did it, like that. [Snaps fingers] (Laughter) There are others I could lay my hand upon and they would go home and say, "Well, it was alright but..." Know you what I say? Ah, indeed. Now, with the whole world, where is the world's consciousness? Is it in healing or is it in illness? Is it in peace or is it in war? Is it in love or is it in hate? Is it in unity or difference?

Participant: Yeah, yeah. Thank you.

Gabriel: Indeed. Ah, beloved woman! How be thou?

Participant: Oh, I am fine, thank you.

Gabriel: Good. Need you to put down your speaking box?

Participant: Yes, I think so. Is that better?

Gabriel: Oh, I know not. Ask the one with the ears. (Laughter) [Referring to the sound person with headphones]

Participant: My question is still, not to belabor the healing, but if you are sending absent healing, so instead of doing that, can you send energy to those people that you feel...instead of sending the absent healing all the time, send them energy to use it as they can?

Gabriel: Send them love, beloved woman. Send them love, for love heals all things. You send a healing forth. You proclaim them to be healed in the name of God, for indeed they are. Now, send them love. See them loved of themselves. See them loving themselves into the perfection that they are, for *all* illness is a form of self-condemnation. It is a wondrous way to punish oneself.

Participant: That makes sense.

Gabriel: Indeed.

Participant: Thank you.

Gabriel: You back again? (Laughter)

Participant: Back again. You mentioned about dreaming and when you dream you go away, you come back, your spirit goes away, it comes back, you wake up refreshed and full of energy. This is every night. So, my spirit goes away, it's dreaming, and if I wake up the next morning and I'm tired and it's like I feel I'm tired and I don't feel the same way I felt the day before that, refreshed, what have I been doing? (Laughter)

Gabriel: Indeed, what *have* you been doing? (Laughter)

Participant: I don't know! I don't recall. It's my memory.

Gabriel: Beloved woman, it depends upon where you go. Now, if you go to a place of refreshment and light or you make use of yourself elsewhere for others' benefit, you come back refreshed. If you get locked into the lower astral and you engage in battle, as it were, with the vibrations there, you are going to come back feeling tired and out of sorts, for you have brought back with you the vibrations of where you have been. So, if you wake up on a morn and you are all discom...discombobble...

Participant: Discombobulated.

Gabriel: Indeed. If you do this, then you can know that wherever you have been, you have brought back lower vibrations and you need to cast them from you.

Participant: And how do we avoid going to those places?

Gabriel: It is your choice. No one makes you go. If you come back and you think, "Oh, I desire not to go where I was, for I feel not well with myself," then the next time you do not go there. Know you what a nightmare be?

Participant: Yes. I don't have them but yes.

Gabriel: It is when an entity chooses to lay aside the physical form for a night of rest and go into the lower realms where there are error thoughts made manifest in all kinds of gross and terrible ways, and they engage in all of this. Then they come back and they have memories of it and they say, "Oh, behold, I have had a nightmare." That is all it 'tis, is traveling about in the lower realms.

Participant: And when you come back, do you generally have...recall where you were in, say, dreams, if you have a nightmare because of the lower realm was where you were dwelling? Do you have good dreams, grand and glorious dreams of where you were when you were out learning?

Gabriel: Depends if you choose to. You can bring back with you a conscious memory if you want to...or not as you choose.

Participant: Okay.

Gabriel: Indeed. Any others?

Participant: I'd like to ask you about babies or very young children that **catch colds** and things like that. If they haven't...if they are too young to think of something?

Gabriel: Indeed, they are but mother and father are not.

Participant: And so it would manifest through the child?

Gabriel: Oh, indeed. Little babies...the innocence of them is that they have not conceived of illness or any negative condition. But babies sleep a lot and mommy and daddy talk a lot. Auntie comes and talks a lot. Grandma comes, "Oh, baby has nothing over their head. Surely they will catch cold. Better you put little booties on the feet, otherwise they will catch cold." What is going into their little mind?

Participant: Oh, I am going to catch cold.

Gabriel: Indeed.

Participant: Okay, thank you. That answers it.

Gabriel: Anyone else?

Participant: In our healing class, we did various types of healing various ways and I was practicing and attempting to heal myself. Can you tell us the best way to heal yourself? Is it by talking to yourself and affirming...?

Gabriel: Proclaiming your own good health. Knowing that the God of you is manifesting through you in perfect health. Say it many times a day as you need to. Claim it. It is in the *claiming* of it that it becomes manifest.

Participant: Yeah. Well, I think that's what we were doing.

Gabriel: Ah, indeed. Ah, you be related?

Participant: Yes, my sister.

Gabriel: Ah, good this life.

Participant: I would just like to continue with what she said. Oh, I'm drawing a blank. Isn't that strange?

Gabriel: No. (Laughter) I didn't mean, "No, it wasn't strange." I meant it is not possible for the mind to be blank. You are not aware of where the thought has traveled to but it will be back.

Participant: Yeah, where did it go? It'll probably come back, okay. I've studied nutrition and been a healer, I think, without being a healer...you know, like you people are healers, and...

Gabriel: Is there a difference? A healer is a healer, beloved woman, whether it be through substance you place in the physical body or whatever.

Participant: A little different. Well, I'd like to ask about nutrition because I've always...since I studied nutrition and, just from my own experience, have found that sugar has not been the greatest thing for me to take in, although I do eat it. How does that relate to, like, waking up tired. Like, for instance, I have cake, I can wake up very tired. I mean without maybe going into lower astral.

Gabriel: Because your physical body...everyone is different for everyone is created uniquely by the entity who is wearing it. If you perceive that which you call sugar to be harmful to you, then it will be.

Participant: Well, I must say that I've improved.

Gabriel: Know you that there are people upon the earth plane who eat all kinds of things, for they know not any better, and they are in perfect health?

Participant: And they are great, yeah.

Gabriel: Indeed. So, if you perceive something to be harmful, then it will be so. Now, there are things that the physical body is *not* meant to have. The lungs are meant to breathe air, not smog.

Participant: Smoke. Smog or smoke.

Gabriel: Indeed, the same. You would not put some substance in your belly that you knew was going to cause your physical body great pain. The substances that are natural for the human body are fruits, green things, vegetables, nuts, berries. Flesh is not a normal thing for a human being to eat. Have you not looked upon your teeth? They are not tearing teeth; they are grinding teeth. Indeed.

Participant: Could I just ask one more? I just wanted a little advice for my cactus plant that I have sitting by my front window trying to get some sun on it. I'm trying to cure it for my son. The poor thing has had a terrible time and I've been trying to do that every day but now you say I only needed to do it once, right?

Gabriel: Love it. Send it healing once but love it, talk to it, tell it how wondrous it be. Say, "The Lord God of your being is manifesting through you with greenness."

Participant: I've been doing that without realizing I was doing the right thing.

Gabriel: It is resting right now, for it has been greatly traumatized and so it is resting. But send it love. Touch it, touch...

Participant: Okay. It's hard to touch. It's all spiny.

Gabriel: Oh, there are little places you can touch.

Participant: Okay, I'll do that. Thank you.

Gabriel: Ah, beloved entity, how be you and all your herbs?

Participant: How do I know them?

Gabriel: How be you?

Participant: I be fine. (Laughter)

Gabriel: Good, indeed. You are fine.

Participant: I am fine, thank you. Only good things happen to me.

Gabriel: Indeed.

Participant: Can I pose my question?

Gabriel: Indeed.

Participant: We, who have been attempting healing and healing for a long period of time, find that we were repeating it over and over. Now you tell us to only do it once and it works, which I agree with...

Gabriel: Isn't it wonderful that he agrees with me? (Laughter)

Participant: And secondly, I agree with the love aspect of it but since you're emotionally involved and you feel you want to say a little more, how about say, "I bless you and send you love"? Is that acceptable?

Gabriel: Of course! Love is *always* acceptable. You can say to someone a thousand times a day, "Behold, I love you."

Participant: How about a blessing thrown in?

Gabriel: A blessing, calling forth from the heavens whatever you conceive of God to be, to bless, to manifest through.

Participant: Okay. So, I bless you and I send you love.

Gabriel: I bless you and I send you love too. (Laughter) Ah, come forth healer. How be all your patients?

Participant: Oh, they're doing fine. They're doing well.

Gabriel: Indeed.

Participant: I have a question about space travel helping us with healing.

Gabriel: How space travel brings healing?

Participant: How we can learn from traveling to different planets to be better healers?

Gabriel: Oh, that would be a whole afternoon to answer that, for it depends where you travel to.

Participant: I've tried it in my meditation and I was wondering if I was on the right track?

Gabriel: Depends on where you want to go. Know you that the healing, the true healing, is from the Spirit. You do not have to go to other galaxies any more than you have to go to anywhere. Wherever you are, God is, and wherever God is, there is perfect health.

Participant: Okay.

Gabriel: If you wish to travel about, go. You are limitless, you know.

Participant: Okay, thank you.

Gabriel: Have we another? No. Ah, then everyone up on their appendages. We have some grand and wondrous energy, have we not? Can you feel the love in the room?

All: Yes.

Gabriel: Good. Let us all join hands then. Come make a circle. If you cannot make a whole circle, perhaps we can join hands across or up and down or some other way. Is everyone joined? Ah.

All: Yes.

Gabriel: Now, do you recognize the God of you? Do you?

All: Yes.

Gabriel: Do you recognize the God of your neighbor?

All: Yes.

Gabriel: We are all God?

All: Yes.

Gabriel: We *know* this?

All: Yes.

Gabriel: We are in perfect health?

All: Yes.

Gabriel: The neighbor is in perfect health?

All: Yes.

Gabriel: There is only that which is joy and love flowing through us?

All: Yes.

Gabriel: We are perfect in every way? Indeed?

All: Indeed.

Gabriel: So be it.

All: So be it. (Laughter)

Gabriel: Ah. Feel you anything?

Participant: Yes, energy.

Gabriel: Energy?

All: Yes.

Gabriel: Ah, you are all wondrous indeed. Now you may put your appendages back in your chairs. (Laughter) Are we finished? Have you anything further to ask of me ere I take my leave?

Participant: Will you come back again?

Gabriel: If you desire me to. Would you come again if I came? Would you care to learn more?

All: Yes.

Gabriel: Indeed. I love to teach. It has been wondrous for me to be here and to see all of your lights. You are like wonderful rainbows, each of you a different shade, a different hue, each of you adding to the beauty of the other, coming together in the loveliness that you are, in the love that you are, blending, being different, and in your differences, adding to the wondrousness of the whole. Even those of you who do not fully understand, and there are those who do not, your beauty is welcomed and a refreshment to us all. Indeed.

Now, I shall have my take-leave music, if I may? I shall sit Beloved Woman down and I shall see you again. You have a question?

Participant: You said before we could heal anyone else, we have to first heal ourself.

Gabriel: Your thoughts, heal your thoughts.

Participant: And we do that once only?

Gabriel: That is a livingness, beloved entity. It is how you are *living* each moment of your life. Know you what I say? If you are living lovingly and if you are cursing not, if what comes forth from you is constructive, life-sustaining, givingness, taking into you that which is beauty and the truth, then you are living the God of you and you are indeed healed. Understand you my words?

Participant: Thank you.

Gabriel: Indeed. Now do I have my going away music? (Laughter) Ah. Blessed be.

Healing Ourselves
February 7, 1993

Archangel Gabriel: I desire greatly to speak to you this night of healing. While there is a powerful vibration of healing at this time upon your earth and it will remain for a short time before it becomes lighter, that does not mean that after it becomes lighter, there will be no healing. It simply means that at this point in your time, it is more powerful than other times.

And though that many of you here perceive that you are not well in one form or another—some of you are troubled in your physical forms, others in your emotional bodies, and some of you are troubled in your mental bodies. And it is at this time that I desire for you to be made whole and for you to recognize that there is no need for you to perceive yourselves as anything but in perfect health.

First of all, when you came forth from the Father-Mother God as a Spirit force, that force is made in the exact image and likeness of God. That is the God part of you. That is the Christ awareness of you. That is the part of you that knows all things, can do all things. That is the part of you that is perfect in every way.

As you took yourselves in your consciousness

43

away from your awareness of God, you perceived that because you were separated, or *thought* you were separated, that you could not be perfect any longer. And because you perceived that you could not be perfect any longer, you began to create for yourself the problems that have filtered down and manifested in your various bodies.

Now, I know there are some of you here who perceive that you have but the one body and that is your physical form. For those of you who think that, let me explain.

The mind of you is not your brain. Your brain is only the physical instrument of it, just as the body you wear is the physical vehicle through which you operate on a three-dimensional world.

You are Spirit. You are light. You are energy. The mind of you uses a vehicle called a mental body that is merely a concentration of mental energy brought together and held in one place, as it were, so to say, in the area of your physical manifestation.

Now, the mind of you is not limited to the physical part of you in any way or form. I've talked to you about this before. You can be in one place and your mind can be in another and you all have experienced this when you have been present with one person and your mind is elsewhere. You're thinking other thoughts, and you do that a lot in church! (Laughter) Now, the ladies are home baking their goodies and the gentlemen are off on your places where you whip that little round ball with a stick, or wherever.

But the mental body of you is not confined to the physical form of you. It is vaster than that—huge, quite large—but its energies are more concentrated around the physical body that you occupy. In other words, it is joined therein but not confined to it.

The emotional body of you is where your feelings come through, where they are filtered through. Now, the feeling aspect of you is in the solar plexus. That is the dwelling place of the subconscious mind. Your feeling body also interpenetrates your physical form but it is not confined to it. Your emotional body is quite free to roam about. Certainly you are aware of this when you are physically present in one place and your thoughts of love and feeling and concern are somewhere else.

Now, your physical body is a vehicle. Without the life that you give it by occupying it, it is a senseless clod. It has no mind of its own. It is completely without any form of intelligence as you know intelligence to be.

However, the subconscious mind of you governs your physical form. If it did not, you would have to concentrate on your heart to make it beat. You would have to concentrate on your flow of blood to make it go throughout your body. When you eat a meal, you would have to command your stomach to digest it and so on and so forth. The fact that you can do all of these things without giving it any thought proves that the intelligence of the body lies in the subconscious mind of you.

Now, the subconscious mind of you is also that which dictates whether you are well or not because if you perceive yourself to be beleaguered with something, then your physical body is going to give you an ache or a pain or an upset tummy or a headache or some other malady. But when you are in a state of clear mental and pure feeling well, your physical body will respond.

Now, what think you that illnesses be? There are those of you who believe you can pick up germs in the air in places on your earth. Actually, all illness has one source and it matters not what that illness manifests as. The only source of illness is fear. Now there's none of you here who do not have your little army of fears that follow you about and beleaguer you.

Now, fear takes many forms and its most subtle form is that of illness because illness you perceive to be a way out of a situation that you desire no longer to participate in. If you are ill, they cannot—they being your peers, your societies—cannot expect you to perform as you are *supposed* to. So illness is a wondrous thing to hide in.

Illness is also the way that you program your body to leave the earth plane. I don't mean your physical form leaves the earth plane, but *you* do. And a lot of you here perceive that if you are to leave the earth plane, then you most assuredly must do it through some ailment or through some perceived accident. Since there are no accidents, everything is done on purpose, that shoots that theory down! (Laughter)

So your other recourse is to become quite ill to the extent where your physical form cannot be revived. And if you care not to do that, you have a third choice, which none of you here have perceived as yet, and that is that of ascending and taking your body with you. A lot of that going on in India. That is quite a common practice there. Also in Tibet, some places of Africa, some of the bush people in Australia. A lot of your native people have done this for a very long time.

There is a small island on the bottom half of your globe—very tiny, small population there. No place to bury anybody so everyone, when they are tired of staying there, simply ascends. There's no graveyard there. It's been done for so many centuries that no one gives it another thought. They simply do it. But that's another story.

Now, healing is more than making your physical body well. Your physical body will never be well until you have transcended in your consciousness the idea of sickness and death. Know you that you are one of the...probably the only planet in your universe that practices death? All the rest of them have learned how to transcend.

True healing is lifting in consciousness your idea of yourself into a state of awareness where you recognize that you are a divine being, you are Spirit. It is in that consciousness that you transcend all of the error perceptions of illness, of injury, of error thought, and ultimately, of physical death.

Now you say, "But that is not possible to do while upon the earth." Well, it is possible. I just told you there are thousands of people who do it all the while and think nothing of it. Why is it not popular where you dwell? I shall tell you why. In order to lift your awareness to that state of consciousness, there has to be *one thought* that you hold to steadfastly and that is that God is all there is. There is nothing outside of the Father.

Now, that does not mean you must think of God

all the time. Obviously you cannot function in your three-dimensional world if you are thinking only of God, but it does mean that you think of God as being present in and with you every moment of your time. Now you say, "But that is not easy to do." It is as simple as anything, far simpler than the complex mentality that you have developed upon your earth. Now let me explain how it works.

First of all, you have to recognize that your world in which you dwell you have created from the point of view of your five senses. Now think about it. Do you not judge by what you see and hear? Do you not base your opinions upon others and yourself by what you perceive them to be doing or saying or having or accomplishing or whatever? Do you not judge the success of another person by how much money they have, how large a home they have, how big a mode of transportation they own, and who their friends are? Do you not elect into the offices of your government those people who are of wealth and power? Think on this, beloveds, for it is the manner in which you perceive of your world.

In your world money is power. Power is money. Money and power denote success and well-being. It is very seldom that you see what you call your street people walking along and say, "Ah, there goes an enlightened soul." (Laughter) Indeed not. You say, "Ah, there goes a poor, wretched creature. Poor thing. I shall lift them in light." But if one of your illuminous, luminous...what do you call those long...? Beloved entity, what is those long modes of transportation that drives with the...? Limousine. One of those things.

48

When you see one of those going by, do you say, "Ah, poor wretched soul. I shall lift them in light"? Indeed not. You have other thoughts.

So, your world is the world of the material and because it is the world of form, you do not perceive the life essence within the form, but rather you judge by the form. Now when you do that, you are bringing your consciousness down and it is very difficult to deal with a spiritual aspect if you do not lift up as high as you are able to go in your consciousness, because as long as you are surrounded by and locked into form, you are not going to perceive the perfection of the Spirit that is you.

So, how do you live in a world of form and think of God? Very simply. Whatever form you be looking at—whether it is a person, a creature, a mode of transportation, whatever...it matters not—you will realize that it is the life force within that form, that that form is merely the out-picturing of a higher ideal.

Now you say, "But how can a dwelling place or a mode of transportation have life in it?" Name me something that is not made of the materials of your earth. Is Mother Earth a living entity? Indeed, and every particle thereof is a living particle. The cells of your body has life in them and intelligence. The cells within wood, even though the tree be long gone and the wood have a different form, that wood has a life in it.

Now, if you think that not be so, then how think you that you can hold an object in your hand and through the vibrations thereof can tell who owned it or who handled it last? Any of you here not familiar with that? There are psychics about your earth who will hold a piece of your garment or a piece of your jewelry or something and give you what you perceive to be a reading on that. I'm sure most of you here are familiar with that. How think you that that be so if what they are holding has no life in it? Because something is not able to move about does not mean it does not contain life. These beauteous flowers do not move about and yet they are as alive as you and I be.

So, going past form into the *life essence* is recognizing God. It is knowing that God is present everywhere about you. And when you come into the realization that *all things are God* in various and sundry forms, then you begin to raise your awareness away from form and into the essence, and as you come into the essence, you are lifted higher until finally, after a bit, you realize that the essence—the life, the Spirit, whatever you want to call it—is present and in the presence of Spirit there can be no illness, nothing of a negative nature. And therein is where you get rid of your fears.

Beloved Woman asked you in your meditation to think of something that you wanted to be rid of. Well, it was rather interesting to me to look into your auras and to see what you chose to be rid of. Haven't got it yet, have you? Be rid of your perception of fear, for fear is the grandest of illusions. Fear will rob you of your health, of your happiness, of the loves of your life. It will rob you of your ability to *live* if you listen to its voice long enough.

Objects in your world of form—whatever they be that you perceive you desire to own or to have—will give you only a short term of joy. But coming into the fullness of God will give you joy for all eternity. Your little baubles and things that you take your monies and buy will soon bore you and after a bit, you will not remember what you did with them.

But when you have that connectedness with God, your joy knows no end. You walk about the earth in perfect health, in perfect happiness, in perfect love, and in perfect everything because you have made the connectedness of your divine self and you have transcended form and you will come into the knowingness of perfect health.

I can see some of you are confused. What has fear to do with my tummy ache or my backache? A lot.

Tummy aches represent something you find hard to stomach.

Aching backs represent the feeling of being unsupported.

A **headache** represents too many things coming at you at once and you don't feel that you can make adequate decisions.

Trouble with your limbs...fear of going forward.

Trouble with your feet denotes fearing that you have nothing solid upon which you may stand.

Problems with your hands, "What if I don't grasp it well enough?" or the opposite...holding on too tight, not letting go.

Trouble in your viscera denotes your inability to digest and to use good ideas.

Heart trouble... "I am not loving enough. I cannot love. I cannot be loved. It is difficult to love. If

I trust and love, I shall be hurt."

Liver problems...the inability to filter out and get rid of the debris in your life.

And so on and so on and so on. And every single one of those goes back to the same thing, *fear of...*

Shall I hang out my shingle and charge you all twenty-five dollars? (Laughter)

You will note that as changes come in your lives, you will manifest different physical problems. Have you not noticed that when you have a new job or you are about to get married or to get unmarried or whatever, when there is a great change, that your back will bother you and your stomach acts up and you just feel awful?

What about **chronic fatigue**? That's something some of you here are experiencing. I can see it in your auras. Chronic fatigue comes from the idea that there's no time to rest. "I'd better not rest. I cannot rest. If I rest, something will go wrong. Therefore, I must keep going, going, going." And your physical body is saying, "Well, you go right ahead. I shall stay here." And then you will find out that you don't have any energy.

Lack of energy comes from dispersing your energy in too many directions or feeling put upon by others, feeling that you must make everybody in the world happy, never mind how you feel.

Have I covered all the maladies in the room? What do you desire that I answer for you?

Skin problems? Oh, that's an easy one. "Something rubs me the wrong way. I don't like it but I can't say anything about it so I'll hold it all in and after I hold it in just so long, there's no longer any place for me to keep it and so it erupts into skin problems."

Participant: I'd like to know a little bit more about **AIDS** and what is the cause of AIDS and what its role on the planet is today?

Gabriel: Indeed. That is a very good example of fear. From the ethers it was drawn by those who feared the happy...the gay people. (Laughter) Well, it means the same in the ethers. You put a different meaning to it to confuse me! (Laughter)

In the ethers, there was a great fear perpetrated, a fear that being gay, as you call it, is something that is catching. And from that fear there came a desire to greatly eliminate all those who were of that vibration. And so they took an innocent creature and they experimented on it until they had developed a virus that would destroy every part in its body of anything that would defend it from any kind of illness or disease.

Now, the plan was quite elaborate. It was of the same vibration that was rampant upon your earth during your war of number two when the entity, Hitler, and that vibrational rate decided to eliminate the Israel people. It was of that same hatred, that same fear.

When it was brought forth into form and begun, there was great rejoicing among those who had initiated it. However, their rejoicing soon turned upon them, for their fear drew to them the very thing that they were trying to be rid of, and it came back to them in the form of this destructive virus that now is no longer limited to those of a happy...of a gay thinking.

Now, upon your earth this day there is a cure and it will be made known before the end of your perceived year. There is also a vaccine that is coming forth that will come a little later. There is a small country who is already using the vaccine and word of it will be pirated away into other countries. It will first come to England and from England out through the world.

Now, it goes back to the same thing: fear. "What if I become one of them? What if my child is taught to be that?" It is the same thinking that made the people of the world think that it was all right to eliminate a whole race of people.

The elimination of a race of people is something that has plagued your earth for eons of time. The most...the one that was the most successful and very nearly totally successful was with the peoples of your very own country. The native peoples of this country were very nearly entirely exterminated before that terrible thought was stopped.

It will end...and soon. Any others? That took care of it all, eh? (Laughter)

Participant: Sounds like you were saying that other people's fears were causing AIDS and not necessarily a specific individual... [inaudible].

Gabriel: It is the vibration of fear was brought down into any form that will manifest...it has to manifest in a form. Everything does. All thoughts, and especially thoughts with emotion...and hate is a powerful emotion. It is a twisted part of fear. When you hate something, it is usually because you are fearful of it in some form and it will take the form of a dis-ease.

Now, the intent behind the AIDS virus was to

destroy a type of lifestyle. "If it is gone, I cannot be caught in it." That was the thought behind it. Those who fall victim to it have chosen to be so. They have chosen to be the sacrificial lamb, as it were, in order that humankind might wake up to realize there is nothing to fear.

Participant: I was wondering if you could you talk about what causes addictive type behaviors... **addictions** to alcohol or various kinds of addictions?

Gabriel: Indeed. Again it goes back to fear. When an entity perceives that they are not adequate to life, that they are not able to deal with life, that they have to have something to hide behind, something to give them courage, it is then that they become locked into the idea, "Well, if I take this or if I have that, I shall be able to be. I shall be acceptable. I shall be able to speak well. I shall be able to do this. I shall be able to do that." And after a bit, they become so dependent on that crutch that they feel they cannot function without it and it goes back to being afraid to be themselves. And that is what all addiction is: fear of not being who you really are, fear of the world knowing who you really are and "If they know me, they won't like me and so I shall hide behind this or that." All people who are addicted to whatever feel they are better in charge of their life and in charge of the situation if they have whatever it is they are addicted to.

Participant: Do you see that there will be a cure for **cancer**?

Gabriel: Oh, there is a cure for cancer. There has been one for the last decade but if they cure it, beloved woman, indeed, how shall they gain their monies? It is the biggest money maker in the medical profession. In this decade the cure will come forth.

Participant: Where is one to find this cure?

Gabriel: It will come forth. In this decade it will come forth.

Participant: [Inaudible question]

Gabriel: Do you believe in God?

Participant: Yes.

Gabriel: Do you believe that He loves you beyond all things?

Participant: Not always.

Gabriel: Not always. Ah, sinful are you, indeed! (Laughter) Beloved woman, there is no such thing as sin. If you were to approach the throne of God and ask Him what is the greatest sin, He would ask you first of all to explain what sin was.

God loves you totally, absolutely, completely, and without exception, and when you can accept that, there will be no room for fear, for your joy will fill your body.

Participant: Could you demonstrate or tell us how a person using what you said about [inaudible] healing could help another person and do healing for another?

Gabriel: To heal another...first of all, you cannot heal another. You only can heal yourselves. Now before everybody gets panicky and says, "Well, throw out the healers," and don't you move... (Laughter)

Now, to heal another, the person who has the illness or perceived illness has to want to be rid of it. Now they may consciously say they want to be rid of it, but if they are subconsciously feeding it through their fear, they are holding to it.

Now, what a healer is doing is allowing themselves to be a channel for an energy which pours in and lifts up the consciousness of that entity. It is in the lifting up of the consciousness of the entity that the healing takes place. So, when you are working with another, lift them constantly up, up, up and healing will be automatic.

Participant: Somebody mentioned the **eyes**. I know that [inaudible]. I'd like to get rid of these glasses.

Gabriel: First of all, beloved woman, what good do they do you there? (Laughter) [Participant is holding her glasses.]

Participant: These are for reading only. Some people are **farsighted** and some are **nearsighted** and [inaudible] need glasses for reading.

Gabriel: And you desire to get rid of them? If you are farsighted, it is the result of not desiring to see what is at hand, what is close to you. You would rather look...direct your energies elsewhere. If you see only that which is in front of you and cannot see ahead, it is the firm belief that there is no future for you or that it could be beleaguered or painful in some manner. So therefore, it is best to deal only with that which is close and never mind tomorrow for tomorrow may be very difficult.

Participant: I don't want to sound flippant but I have one eye which is farsighted and the other eye is nearsighted. (Laughter) What is even more interesting...I have gone to an ophthalmologist for quite a few years and all of a sudden she said, "Oh my god, your eyes have flipped. The one which was nearsighted became farsighted." (Laughter) Could you explain that?

Gabriel: Indeed. That is rather a common malady, you know. And that is a person who is extremely busy, who is able to do many things at the same time who very rarely has one job or one profession or whatever, who is sort of a jack of all trades...is able to do many things well. Therefore, their vision is on what they are doing and what they are going to be doing tomorrow. You are the type of person who can be doing this and your mind is off on something else, are you not? Now, the fact that they turned around the other way is a very interesting phenomena because that denotes a great change in your thinking at the time.

Participant: There was a change in my life.

Gabriel: Indeed. A change of how you looked at life.

Participant: My grandfather had a **stroke** and is barely present. What happened?

Gabriel: When there is a stroke, it is usually because the entity is desiring greatly to leave the earth...on the one hand. On the other hand, they are fearful of what they would find if they leave the earth. In other words, they fear death. Through a stroke, they are taken out of life but they do not experience death, so therefore they are safe in their mind. They are safe.

When an entity recovers from what you term to be a stroke, it is usually because they have decided...they have come to realize they have not finished with their earthly things as yet and therefore they must continue on for yet a little longer. When they leave through stroke, it is because their fear of death is gone and they know it is all right for them to go on.

Paralysis usually comes from an overwhelming

fear. I can't move. I dare not move. I'd better not. When one is deprived of the ability of **speech**, it is because they are fearful of saying something. "If I say something, I shall cause trouble. They shall be angry with me. Therefore, better I am silent."

If you will think of what your problem be and think of how it is manifesting in your life, you can pretty well figure out why you have it and you can be rid of it.

Participant: I feel like asking you about every problem and illness that my friends have.

Gabriel: How much time have you got? (Laughter)

Participant: You have eternity!

Gabriel: Indeed, I do! (Laughter)

Participant: I had an issue of **narcolepsy**, which is very perplexing. By the way, does every person with narcolepsy have it for the same reason?

Gabriel: Depends. Not always the exact reason but very similar reasons.

Questioner: They say it runs in families.

Gabriel: Indeed, because people of a like thought pattern usually draw together to form a family. There are very strong similarities in dealing with life in families. A lot of similarities there.

Participant: I've had it worse before and there is no explanation that I know of. [Inaudible]

Gabriel: Beloved woman, why think you that you fear to stay upon the earth? It comes a fear of tomorrow. "It is better to slip away while I can," type of thinking. Now, it is not a conscious thought...a fear that you cannot please or that you cannot measure up to another, especially a family member usually. Does that clarify it for you?

Participant: That's quite insightful, thank you.

Gabriel: Indeed. If I wouldn't open a Pandora's Box, I could tell you exactly who and when and where but I would not because then I'd have a roomful of people up here. (Laughter)

Participant: My mother's high standards and her competitiveness?

Gabriel: Indeed. (Laughter)

Participant: Thank you.

Participant: I have one part—and this seems like an awfully vain question—but I have one part of my body, this little part, that seems that no matter how much I physically exercise, how much I eat the right things, it stays the same size. (Laughter) How...

Gabriel: Beloved entity, look around you. (Laughter) You are not alone. (Laughter) Now, the **tummy** and that area of the body represents that which is taken in and digested and used, and everyone in the earth plane always desires to take in more than what they really need and so it builds up.

How to get rid of it? (Laughter) Simply say to your physical form, "You are in perfect health, perfect weight, perfect dimensions." It's that simple.

Participant: Good evening. When a doctor says to you that your **disease is hereditary** and you have seen other people in your family and one is lucky enough to have it with you, how does something like this manifest?

Gabriel: Lucky enough?

Participant: Well, you have it. Or unlucky, whatever you want to say. You're two out of ten so you know, you're doing something either right or wrong.

Gabriel: You are doing something wrong, indeed. Well, you're not doing anything wrong; you've chosen to do it. But the simple explanation is that when a family group decides to incarnate together and they all decide who is going to play what part—you be Daddy, you be Mommy, I'll be little brother, and so on and so forth—they also bring with them the vibrational rate of their unified thinking and feeling. This is what I said to the other entity, that there is always a common ground in families. They either think alike or they feel alike or there is a lot of similarities there.

Now, that which you are manifesting in your form comes from the feeling that there was not enough sweetness in your life. "I cannot give off enough sweetness. I am not sweet enough."

Participant: The weird part about this whole thing is the brother that has the same problem I have...we are totally different.

Gabriel: On the surface, indeed, but there is that underlying similar feeling, "I am not sweet enough."

Participant: I'd like to ask something about **breast cancer**. [Inaudible]

Gabriel: [Inaudible] ...is a problem with the organs of reproduction, regardless of whether it be male or female. The entity is questioning their right to create. Now, with the breasts, that usually denotes an entity who feels that she cannot go on nurturing any longer because she is not being nurtured herself and she has nothing left to give. And for it to be manifested in her life, she has to be rid of the organs of nurturing, which, in the female, would be the breasts.

Now, the cure, as you call it, for that would be to recognize that she is not responsible for nurturing the world. She is only responsible for nurturing herself and she doesn't have to concern herself about her breasts to nurture herself.

Participant: This is basically a curiosity question but since you opened up the door on vanity. I have to ask, is there anything that can be done about **baldness**, as far as males or females go?

Gabriel: What be baldness? Oh, no hair.

Participant: Thinning of the hair.

Gabriel: Well, there are those here who don't seem to be bothered by it! (Laughter)

Participant: But there are a lot who are...

Gabriel: First of all, it comes from the idea that, "I am a very honest people and I shall hide nothing from the world." Now, they may not be honest but they think they are and they do not desire to hide anything. Does that make sense to you?

Participant: No, it doesn't. Honest person? I am.

Gabriel: I'm not saying that you are not but the person who is troubled by this wants to project that to the world that they have nothing to hide and hair can hide a lot of things.

Participant: This is probably the only part of the body you hadn't touched on. The mouth and the structures around your **mouth**.

Gabriel: The structures of your mouth...

Participant: Not your teeth. Your **gums**, and the bone around it.

Gabriel: The structures of your face then.

Participant: Okay, but more around your mouth.

Gabriel: The mouth is interesting part of the physical form because it is one of the few places in which something can come forth from it and something is put in to it, and a person who does not put food into their mouth soon starves. A person who is reluctant to speak out, to give [inaudible], as it were, is someone who feels they are fearful of what will happen if they speak.

Now, the Master Jesus said, "Do not concern yourselves with what you put in your mouth but it is out of the mouth that the issues of the heart are known." So a person who would have trouble with the structure around there would have a great deal of difficulty with feeling comfortable expressing what they really feel.

Participant: When you talked about all of these reasons tonight, do you feel that some people may not be able to identify with them?

Gabriel: Oh, I'm sure. I'm sure. Because if the ego allowed them to understand, they couldn't be rid of their fear.

Gabriel: Hello beloved soon-to-be woman. (Laughter)

Participant: How do you deal with **allergies** and **infections**?

Gabriel: Allergies and infections. First of all, let me find out what they be. (All right) An allergy is something...usually it is an outer manifestation of an inner feeling that you are not in tune with your environment. You are not in tune with where you are. Not just in your physical environment but in your consciousness. You are not in tune with where you are.

63

Now, infection is when you are holding something inside of you and you're not going to let go of it. You're not willing to release it and let it go so it's going to stay there and fester. This usually comes down to not expressing anger.

Now, are you going home and punch your little brother? (Laughter) Better not.

Participant: Based on what you said about people getting together and having the same fears, and then they come to earth as family, much is said in science about **genetics**. Are you suggesting that there's not a genetic component, as far as the genes in the body passing it on? Because we all agree or because we agree with the fears but the genes are created from that fear?

Gabriel: That is the answer there because when... Don't forget, you create your physical body before you enter it. So, you would bring into the cells of that body or into the genes, as you say, those fears, which are going to manifest. And that is why it is what you call, "runs in families," as it were, because that thought, that vibration, is brought right into the etheric body, which of course creates the physical body and all of it is just pictured out there.

Participant: Okay, I have a follow up question then. The gentleman said that in a large family, there were two of them that had [inaudible] and the rest of them did not. In my family there was a problem that permeated the whole family but sometimes one in eight or one in nine would have a problem and not the rest.

Gabriel: When there is a single individual who has a

problem, it is usually because they are bringing it forth as a lesson to the others in the family.

This is the last one, for we are over your perceived time. Indeed.

Participant: Just a question about the **prostate gland**.

Gabriel: There again you are going into the creative force. It is there that the creative force is being choked off, not allowed to flow, so therefore there will come a strangulation of that.

I shall send you my bill in the morn! (Laughter) And I shall bid you a fond farewell and I shall see you all again soon.

Divine Light, that is the light of all life,
we ask that these, Thy beloved children,
be lifted up in awareness into that light
so that they might realize the unity they have with
You,
with each other, with all life.
Bless them, Father God, in their awareness
that they may leave behind their fears
and bring forth into manifestation
that perfection in which they were created.
This we ask and know
as it is asked, it is done.
So be it.

Questions & Answers
February 13, 1996
Selected Section on Physical Ailments

Participant: Several of us have had **infections** and my sense about infections is that they represent a festering or rotting away of the old that no longer is valid or that no longer works for us.

Archangel Gabriel: That is partially true. The other part of an infection is when you feel invaded by a foreign element, when you feel that your power is being usurped by something outside yourself that has entered into your space where it has no right to be.

Participant: But that's not true?

Gabriel: No, it isn't true. It's part of the victim complex.

An infection in any part of the body, if you will take note of the part of the body, will give you a good idea of where you feel...what area of your life you feel has been invaded, and there is a lot to be said for paying attention to what your body tells you.

Now, an **infection in the head**, in your **sinuses** and that kind of thing, usually means that you feel overwhelmed. You have more things to do than you feel you have adequate time or energy to take care of, and you frequently feel beleaguered or put upon by others. In other words, they have invaded your space. The sinuses are empty spaces. Didn't know you all had empty heads, eh? (Laughter) But the thing is that when that aspect of you becomes infected, then you can know that you feel someone else has invaded your space.

The **throat**...that is your power center and when you have trouble with that, you can know that you feel that someone else is taking your power, or you are giving away your power to someone or something else. Sometimes it is a situation. Sometimes it is an individual.

When you have trouble with your **lungs** with taking in air or expelling air, that usually denotes an attitude that, "I don't have a *right* even to have the breath of life," or an attitude of "Life is leaving me and I can't take it *in* anymore."

When you have **tummy** troubles, it is usually because you are refusing to digest information that *you* know brings a truth to you that will require of you to expel or get rid of something that can no longer serve you. After all, your food goes into your stomach, is processed there, feeds your body, and then is expelled. But when the stomach and intestines refuse to do that, it is because you're *hanging on* to the debris that you need to release and let go of.

Your body will always tell you what's going on in your nature, in your subconscious mind. It will always tell you what is going on. The stress that people live in on your earth today has produced illnesses that were never heard of several hundred years ago and it is because you are not meant to live at the pace that you live. Years ago, people rose early, worked hard all day, and went to bed early. Now they rise early, work hard all day, and go to bed late. Don't eat half of the time. When they do, they eat in cardboard and sawdust flavored with...what is it? Ketchup? (Laughter)

She [Tinkerbell] likes the word "ketchup." She was going around the other day saying, "Ketchup, ketchup, ketchup." (Laughter) I said, "What are you saying?" She said, "Ketchup." I said "What is that?" She said, "It's an earth word." I said, "What does it mean?" "I don't know but isn't it fun. Ketchup, ketchup, ketchup!" (Laughter) Now she is going around singing, "Ketchup!" Now she's told all the little cherubs, "Ketchup, ketchup." Are we hearing songs now of loveliness? No, we are hearing little ditties about ketchup. (Laughter) So I said to her, "If you're going to sing about it, you better find out what it is," and she was quite disappointed that it was some kind of sauce or other. She thought it was something more exciting apparently. But she's delightful anyway.

Participant: Gabriel, you had said a couple of times ago about asking for healing and accepting that it's coming. And then I spoke to Reverend Ellen yesterday and she had talked about paying attention to things that cross my path, and it's been an interesting kind of thing that's happened. I see it as a great big puzzle to be solved and little pieces of the puzzle are being solved from meditation or a note somebody gives to me or a telephone call someone makes. And I just...I guess I want verification that I am doing okay.

Gabriel: You are doing very well, indeed. Have you

not had a lot of insight?

Participant: Yes, a lot. It's almost been exciting.

Gabriel: Yes, and it will be even more exciting when the last piece of the puzzle is in place and then you say, "Ah, praise God. Now I know the answer."

Participant: Could we speed that part up a little bit? (Laughter)

Gabriel: Well, it is up to you. You go at your own pace. We always allow you to go at your own pace. We never hurry you along. Well, once in a while we give you a little push, but everyone has their own pace, their own rate of vibration through which they work best, and whatever teaches you, we leave alone. If you're learning from it, we let it be. Sometimes it's hard to find something you learn from, you know, and when we do, we don't fool around with it. If it isn't broke, we don't fix it. (Laughter)

Participant: What about **teeth**?

Gabriel: Teeth represent your ability to really get into the finer things, for your teeth grind up your food so that it might be palatable to you when swallowed. So it is a matter of you going through and sorting out and crunching down, as it were, the details that would be feeding you and giving you energy, new ideas and so forth. And when one hangs on to a bad tooth through fear, one can pretty well know that one is hanging onto old pain, because the future is very unstable in your mind.

Participant: I got rid of a tooth today. (Laughter)

Gabriel: And now, beloved entity, you shall find that another issue in your life, which has troubled you from time to time—one that you could shove aside and then it would come out and you'd you push it back—will also come to its own conclusion and you won't have to deal with it anymore.

Notice how so many of you are beleaguered with **stuffy noses** and...what do you call that...**sinus problems**?

Participant: You said that that was...that we feel that we are overwhelmed and take on more than we could handle.

Gabriel: That is true.

Participant: Could this maybe be a lesson in patience?

Gabriel: Patience, and also in learning to discern that which is necessary for you and that which is not.

Participant: Those of us who are trying to juggle our time, balance our time, in between different things and find ourselves missing things that we want to be at or something else that we feel we have...priorities I guess. Trying to find priorities.

Gabriel: What is the most important thing to you?

Participant: My spirituality is the most important thing to me.

Gabriel: Indeed, but you must earn a living, so you think, eh?

Participant: Yes, I have to live in this world.

Gabriel: That is true. Now, how think you that you can balance that?

Participant: Well, I made sure that I could make it here, at least.

Gabriel: First of all, beloved entity, change your attitude. Do not think of the method in which you earn your living as a robber, a thief who steals away your spiritual opportunities, and you will find that the cooperation that you require will *just miraculously happen*. But when you regard one aspect of your life as an antagonist or an enemy, then you have engaged in battle and it will never be easy. But when you see all things working together in a cooperative manner, you will be amazed at the things that will unfold for you. There is no thief excepting in your own mind.

Participant: So it's merely looking at it as a blessing and not as something that has to be done.

Gabriel: Indeed.

Participant: What about **headaches**?

Gabriel: Ooo...the headaches. We've been around the barn with that one with Beloved Woman. "Some angels you are. I can't get rid of a headache. What good are you!?" (Laughter)

Participant: I didn't blame it on you.

Gabriel: Oh well, she does. You know, I'm to blame for everything, from indigestion to the cat getting out. (Laughter) However, to answer your question...

Headaches usually occur through tension. When you feel you have to be too many different directions doing too many different unrelated things, then is when tension builds up. Now, the vessels in the brain and up through the head... Your head will bleed much more so than any other part of your body with exception of your heart because you have a lot of blood vessels, and when you become anxious, overwhelmed, those blood vessels constrict. And the headache is caused by the blood trying to get through their natural avenues.

Now what this boils down to is when something is

to be done through its natural avenue and you are *resenting* it, you will result in a headache because you're constricting the natural avenues of movement and it will manifest as a constriction of the blood vessels in your head and that produces pain. Make a lot of sense to you?

Participant: Oh, yes.

Gabriel: I thought so.

Participant: What about problems with legs and the feet?

Gabriel: Feet represent your ability and willingness to understand, and when you are having foot trouble, it is usually because you are being rather rigid or unyielding in something that would require your understanding. Not necessarily agreement, but understanding.

The **legs** represent your ability to propel yourself forward and when your movement forward becomes painful, it is because you feel that anything that requires you to change or move from the spot you're in would not be good, and therefore be painful to you. So it manifests in painful legs.

Besides, if you are referring to yourself, which I feel you are, you're on your feet entirely too much. You need to get some help and semi-retire. You've earned it. And that is a grand truth. There are places to go, people to see, things to do. Why stay you always there to fuss with some lady's hair?

Participant: Beloved Gabriel, she's always on the go. Even though she's on her feet doing that, she's still running all over the place.

Gabriel: But wouldn't it be better to run on feet that

were cooperative and legs that didn't hurt you? Would it not be better?

Participant: Probably.

Gabriel: I rest my case. (Laughter)

Participant: But I like what I do.

Gabriel: Oh, I didn't say you didn't, but I think you need more time for you...to do whatever.

Participant: Why do we have to suffer these physical infirmities, these physical equivalents that we are talking about, in order to learn these lessons? Couldn't we learn them some other way? Or aren't we spiritually evolved enough to circumvent the physical infirmities from happening?

Gabriel: [Pointing up] Now, You see! I'm not the only one with that question! Beloved woman, we have spent more millions of years than your minds could comprehend asking the same thing of you humans. Why do you do these things to yourselves?

Participant: Why? Why do we?

Gabriel: We don't know. It seems to be this peculiar thing you have for suffering. We get you out of one thing and we think, "Well, there, that's that," and plop in you go with another. There is no reason for physical suffering. There's no reason for suffering of any kind. That's all human created and we have often marveled at your ability to create such awful things for yourselves, awful things for you to go through, and when you've been through them, we think, "Well now, perhaps they've learned they don't like that." And you think, "Oh, that was awful. Did you see what I went through?" "Yes I did. It was terrible, terrible indeed." "Oh, I shall never go through that again." "Oh, I don't think you should ever but I heard of another thing that is twice as bad. Would you like to try that?" (Laughter) "Oh yes, I think I shall! Where is it?" And off you go. And we think, "There you go."

All through the eons of time, if you look back through your histories, can you *imagine* creating some of the terrible things that you've created and put yourselves through? It's absolutely amazing. We frequently sit around and discuss the perplexities of humankind and we thank God that we are not one of you (laughter) because we're always happy. We enjoy what we do. We love life, and we don't ever create anything that is unhappy, even Tinkerbell with her ketchup. She had a grand time with it. Played all over heaven with that.

But you don't know how to *play* with your creativity. You always create something dastardly for yourselves instead of something joyous. Instead of creating suffering, why not create harmony? Instead of creating loneliness, why not create love and unity? It wouldn't take half as much effort. Do you realize the energy you expend in creating something terrible? Because it's contrary to life, absolutely contrary to life. So I can't answer you, beloved woman. I thought perhaps you would be wiser than I in that. (Laughter)

Participant: There's a song called, "That will be the day." (Laughter)

Gabriel: Indeed.

Participant: You told us once that it took about six months for an illness to work from the etheric body to the physical.

Gabriel: It depends on the illness but that is

approximately the time it takes. Of course, some illnesses...it depends on the temperament of the person, you know. A lot of people release something and before it can be completely gone, they pull it all back again. And they wear it for a day or two and then they release it again, and it depends on how many times they yank it back as to how long it takes.

For example, there was a little lady who had arthritis in her legs very bad, and she was having a great deal of difficulty getting about so she went to a faith healer and she was truly healed. And she was so excited. She went home and she called her sister and she related the whole incident to her. And then the next day, she called another, and another, and by the end of the week, she had the arthritis back because she kept saying, "Remember when I couldn't walk and remember this and remember that?" and she reminded herself consistently in telling others what a painful thing she'd been through until she had pulled it all right back again by talking about it.

And people do that. They really do. Instead of telling, "I am free of pain. Isn't it wonderful? I am going to do thus-and-so," she recounted the years and years of her suffering and surely indeed, she called it all back. That's what happens when people receive a healing, and then a few weeks later, the illness or ailment has returned. It is because they have recounted it over and over and drew it back. So don't do that, beloved woman. Let your ailment just fly off.

Participant: When I'm using myself as an example, talking about some habits that I had in the past or behavior patterns that I no longer have to someone else, I'm not calling that back, am I?

Gabriel: Not unless you do it with the idea of allowing them to see how terribly you suffered. In other words, beloved entity, let us say that you had a habit of stepping in front of modes of transportation to see whether you could collect a sum of money if they run over you. (Laughter) What do you call that?

Now, you got run over several times, no doubt. Now, if you were to tell of it from the perspective of how clever you were to devise the little scheme, rather than to say, "Oh, I had a terrible back injury. I had a terrible cranial injury. I had broken my arm," and all that sort of thing. Now, if you were to get into the *pain* of it, then you would pull that back. But if you were to get into the cleverness of it, not that I think stepping in front of modes of transportation is particularly clever (laughter)...but it depends on how you use the example.

In fact, most things people do are not very clever at all. I mean in terms of negative things, I'm saying.

Healing in the World
March 28, 1998

This lecture was given at Fellowships of the Spirit in Lily Dale, New York to a group about to graduate from their course of study to become ministers.

Archangel Gabriel: You are going forth into a world that is rapidly changing and you are going forth almost as strangers in a strange land because you are bringing in a spiritual light, you are bringing in a truth that the average person doesn't know exists, or if they know of it, they are fearful of it or they do not believe it. And so as you go forth as teachers and healers, as counselors, as helpers, you are going forth into an atmosphere that could appear to you at times to be rather unfriendly. I know most of you here are very comfortable with what you are doing and most of you have reached the point where you don't care whether your neighbor likes it or your family agrees or not, you do it. But you still will be encountering people who will challenge you, challenge your beliefs, challenge how you know these things. "If this is a truth, then why doesn't the world know it?" and that kind of thinking. So it is important for you to be firmly established in what you know and what you believe and what is your path.

Now even though you all have studied with the same teacher and have learned these truths from a very fine source, you still are going to take these truths into the world in a way that is particular to you because you are going to be filtering what you have learned through your own spiritual selves and that alters it a little bit. Each of you is a little different from the other and that's how it's supposed to be. If all the notes of a musical instrument were the same, there would be no harmony, so you are all intended to be lights in the world and the glow of your light is a little different than the glow of your neighbor's light.

Do not ever be afraid to be who you are because that is one of the things that spiritual teachers and people on the path frequently run into. As soon as a challenge comes along, they become afraid to be who they are. Some of them will compromise what they know in order to fit in or to be accepted. Others will think that everybody else knows more than they do or they will meet another teacher and they will think, "Oh, I had best keep still because he or she knows far more than I and I don't want to appear a fool." Never ever feel that you have nothing to offer or that what you have to offer is not as good as the next fellow's.

Now, I am saying this to you for a reason because we have been about among you. Your guardian angels report back to us whenever we are going to speak before a group. I like to know what you think, how you think, how you feel about yourselves, what you have learned, how far you are along... That tells me what I can teach you. And so I've had all these reports come in from your guardian angels and your teachers. You are all pretty smart fellows. (Laughter)

However, among you we have found...there seems to be a feeling of uncertainty as to just exactly what you are supposed to be doing. It's like last eve, we came and visited with you and you were lying there in your beds and you're thinking, "Oh, tomorrow we go and hear Gabriel. I hope he tells me what I'm supposed to do with all this stuff." (Laughter) Because you don't seem to *know* what to do with it.

We are never allowed to interfere in your free will, you know, short of saving you from falling off a cliff or something, but we are allowed to give you insight into your journey, into the path that you have chosen, and so forth, and that's what we are going to do this day. We are going to give you a sense of direction.

First of all, one of...no, not one of...*the* most important thing for you to know and to never ever forget, no matter what, is that you are a spiritual being. You don't become spiritual when you die. When you die, you become dead, but while you are living, which is forever, you are a spiritual being. And this body that you occupy and the journey that you have chosen for yourself upon this earth is a grand and wondrous dream that you create as you go along, and you can have in it anything that you want, anything. Now, when I say anything, I'm not talking about fancy cars or palatial homes or something like that, or all the wealth in the world. I am talking about the experiences that allow you to demonstrate, to yourself first of all and then to others, your highest and best self, which is your image and likeness of God. "Oh," but you say, "I don't know that part of me."

[Gabriel draws a figure.] This up here we are going to say is your Spirit Self, your God Self. Now, I am going to use the color green because all of you are healers, even those of you who think you aren't, and you are all teachers, even those of you who think you don't know what to teach and therefore you're not a teacher. So, we are dealing with healing, which is green, and we are dealing with the intellect, which is yellow.

Now, upon the earth you all appear normal. A person looking upon any of you would not say, "Ah, behold, there is a teacher, there is a healer, there is a weird person." (Laughter) So here you have your earthly body and you go about your earthly business, but in the secrecy of your internal self, there is this divine love, which comes from up here, filters in, mixes in with this, and comes in and affects your earthly life.

Now, when you are dealing with earthy things, earning your living and so on and so forth, you are pretty much down in here all the time. You're down in the earthy part of you. However, when you meditate and when you prepare to do your healing and your teaching, you aren't down any longer. You automatically shift gears, as it were, and you go up into your healing, teaching self.

When someone down here asks of you something of a spiritual nature—whether it be to counsel them or to give them a healing or to teach, whatever—you bring your information down into *their* world. You do not take *their* vibration up into *your* world, and I shall tell you why.

Anything of a lower nature...when I say lower, I don't mean someone who is evil or something. I am not talking about that. I am talking about someone who is uninformed, someone who is not consciously on the path of spirituality. So, they are very heavy down in here [draws] and you don't want that heaviness up in your spiritual mode. You don't want that up there. You want to stay as pure and as clear as you can up in here [draws].

So, you pull from the Spirit Self of you—and we shall give you an exercise to do so you know how to do that—you pull from up here and you bring that information down into your teaching/healing mode. And it is from *that* aspect of you that you work. That mixes in with what you are saying, what you are doing, and you bring *that* down into *their* world.

Let me give you an example. Let us suppose that someone comes to you and they're very distressed, terrible situation in their life, they are very heavy with despair. What good would you be to them if you came down and entered into their despair?

They didn't come to you for you to pat them on the back and say, "There, there. Poor dear. I know how you feel. This is awful. That wretched person doing this to you. Ta da da da." That is not helping them. So you don't take their problem up. You bring your solution to it down.

Now, here is a little exercise that you can do. When someone comes to you for advice or healing and they are extremely distressed, the first thing you do is put the white light of protection around yourself. Now, I'll tell you what happens when someone comes to you in a great need. You are the source of light. They are in darkness. They will find your light—that's why they came to you—and they will pull your energy from you.

How many of you have given a healing or given counseling and afterwards you felt totally drained? You just felt *so* exhausted. That should not be because your Source is up here and the spiritual Source of your beingness can never be depleted, ever. You are eternal and that source of strength—for healing or counseling, whatever—is *forever* and it never diminishes. No matter how much you use it, it never, ever becomes lesser.

So what happens when this person has done this to you? I can tell you. You have allowed their sorrow, their heaviness, to come up into this very sacred area of you.

Let me tell you a little secret, although I don't know how secret it is. When you enter upon the path to teach or to heal, as you go, you develop from the *within* of you a kind of a shield that goes around you and the longer you work, the greater the shield, the greater the light, the further out it reaches until finally people like Buddha, the Master Jesus...their field of energy was several miles wide. That is why when the Master walked through villages, people were healed who didn't even see him, because of his energy field.

It becomes a part of your aura and people who are not consciously on the path of healing or counseling don't have one. So you have all begun when you first said, "I think I want to go to the partnership..." What is your name? Not partner...Fellowship. I knew it had a togetherness thing. (Laughter) Now, when you first said, "I am going to the Fellowship," that was when that little light began—a little, tiny light, big as the end of her finger—that is when it began. And as you read books, as you studied, as your desire grew, that light grew and grew. As you studied, as you learned, as you practiced on one another, your lights grew and grew and grew, and as you go out into the world, they will grow and grow.

Now, that light is right here between your spiritual Source and the world into which you are going to be working. It is a field of energy that never leaves you. You've all got it as I sit there looking at you. You've all got this glowing light around you, some of you more than others, but all of you have it. Teacher back there has a great wide one. Healer back there has another. You all have this.

Now, those people who come to you from their desperation cannot, *should* not, be allowed into that field of energy without your permission and I shall tell you why. It is at that point that they can draw that energy. They go away from you feeling wondrous indeed and you feel like yesterday's lunch.

Now, the power you have in that energy field is your holy, sacred, private stuff. It is not just to be given out indiscriminately.

Know you the story of when the Master Jesus was walking through the crowd and the woman with the issue of the blood reached out and touched his garment, and he stopped and he said, "Who touched me?" And Peter said, "What are you talking about who touched you? You are in a crowd of people bumping and jostling. What are you talking about who touched you?" He knew. He felt and he knew that she had touched into his holy space. She didn't know she did, but he did, he knew it, and she pulled energy and she was healed like that.

Now, lest you think he is the only one who does that, everyone who teaches spiritual things, true spiritual things... I am not talking about your charlatans. I am talking about the true, the sincere, everyone who heals. How many of you in here do healing? Oh... (Laughter) All hands should be up! Where was your hand? All of your hands should be up.

You know, there is something you must realize. When you enter upon the spiritual path, you don't have a choice whether you are going to be a healer or not. That goes with the territory. (Laughter) That's a grand truth. When you began to teach, you are healing.

Beloved Woman has always said to me, "Oh, but I'm not a healer. I don't think I am a healer. I'm not a healer." I said, "What do you think the words that come out of your mouth do?" "Oh," she said, "I didn't think of that."

So when you speak a truth, when you lay on hands, whatever you do, you are healing. And the words you use, the lessons you give, they are as powerful a healer as the laying on of hands, and don't forget that.

What is your purpose in the world? Is it not to heal the world? And you start with the first person you encounter and that's you. So, lest we get off on another track here...

When you are working with someone distressed, bring your spirituality *to their problem* because you keep the energy...in that way you are pulling the energy into your sacred space and you are allowing it out, with your permission, in the amount that is needed to heal them and not anything further than that.

Now, the strange thing about people—and they don't know they're doing this at all—when they have a need, they *pull* all of the energy they can get a hold of. They're like a drowning person grabbing onto something to keep from going under, and they will hold and pull and hold and pull until they have drained you, until there is nothing.

Now the thing is, when you give out from your holy space knowledgably, you are going to heal. You are going to counsel. The only amount that comes out is the amount needed at the moment for the problem. Nothing more. That person cannot pull all that you've got from you, and you will not be depleted and you will not feel tired.

However, here are all these lovely little students with your hearts on their sleeve and the first thing that pops into your mind when someone says, "Oh, I have a dreadful headache," is, *"Oh, let me heal you."* (Laughter) Or someone says, "I don't know what I am going to do with my mate. He is fighting me." *"Let me help you."* So what are you doing? You're opening the flood gates of your sacred space and you are *giving away your power*, your energy.

Now, there is a way of helping, a way of healing, *that doesn't take all you've got* and that's what we're going to teach you today.

Let us suppose someone comes to you with a cancer and they tell you they have a great fear. They have cancer. They don't want to go through the agony of it. They don't want to die. They don't want to leave their family. How is their family ever going to pay for all of the treatments? And so forth.

And they say to you, "I know you do spiritual work. Will you heal me?" What would your response be? Every single one of you would say, "Of course. Come. Sit. Let me give myself away to you." No. You don't help them and you don't help yourself.

So, here's what you do. You say to them, "I desire greatly to help you. Just give me a few moments." Just sit quietly and if it's possible, take yourself into another room away from them. Now, they are very needy sitting there so they are like a great sponge, all these little hands reaching out to grab from you. They don't mean it. They don't even know they're doing it. Take yourself into another room or at least away from them.

Now you go up into your Spiritual Self. You may be thinking, "I don't know how to do that." Well, we're going to teach you how to do that. You go up into your Spiritual Self and you say to *their* Spiritual Self... Now this is the important part. You have to communicate on the *highest* possible level. You don't want to talk to the personality self. The personality self is caught in fear and in pain and in great distress so you're not going to get any kind of a clear answer there. You go up to their Spiritual Self and you say to their Spiritual Self, "The personality is experiencing great fear and disease of the body. I do not know your journey. Is this part of the journey? Have you elected to walk that path of pain and fear? Or have you elected rather to change your mind and not go through that experience at all but rather recognize that you are a child of God and you don't need to do that?" Now, you don't have to use these exact words. You formulate your own. It must come from your heart. And then you listen.

Everyone chooses their own path before they come to the earth. You know that. And everyone has the right to change their mind at any point along the way. And you don't know what they have chosen. You don't know what lessons they have elected to experience. So therefore, to be the finest, best help to them, you must ask permission from the Spirit Self of them. You must say to them, "What do you want me to do? Do you want me to comfort, take away pain, and let them walk their way or do you want them to be healed? What is your plan?" And then listen and with *no* exceptions, you will be given the answer. You will *know* what you are supposed to do with this person.

Once you have that established... Let us suppose the answer comes back...they have changed their mind. They want to live. They want to be healed. Now you know. You come back and you are going to heal them. Now, let me rephrase that. You are going to give them energy to work with and they are going to heal themselves because that's what happens, you know. You are the mediator. The power is God's. You are the director and they are the receiver. What they do with

89

it has nothing to do with you and has nothing to do with God. It has to do with their willingness to take it in and to utilize it. Some people use it to pass over into spirit painlessly. Some people use it to heal the cells of the body and to be restored in their completeness to perfect health.

Now, you go back into the room and you say to the person, "We're going to work with your fear." "Oh, I don't need to work with that. I need to work with the cancer." "No, we're going to work with your fear because that produced the cancer. We're going to work with your rejection of life. You are rejecting life. That's why you are letting your fear eat you up. So we are going to start working with your fear."

Then you start the healing process beginning not with the body. The body is only the out-pictured end result. You're going to start working with them up in their Spirit and you're going to talk to them from your higher self and you're not going to mind what comes out of your mouth because you will be amazed at what you say. You are going to think, "I wonder how I knew that."

They will respond to you because you are speaking *truth*. They may at first say, "Well, I don't know what you're talking about." That's the fear, but within they're saying, "Thank you, Father, for these words of healing and hope," always from the Spirit downward through your sacred space and into their world. And in this way, the healing takes place.

Now you must remember, the body will do exactly what it's told. If it is told to be pain-filled, if it is told to deteriorate and to die, that's what it's going to do. If it is told to be well, to be vitally alive, that's what it will do. That's how miraculous healings happen. It isn't any power outside of the body. It is the power within the Spirit of the individual *in* that body and that is how healing is brought about.

Now you as a healer, your job is to be in touch with your own sacred space. How many of you here feel that you know how to get to and are familiar with your sacred space? Not too many of you. Have you ever had it happen that a puzzlement presented itself to you, a situation presented itself to you that was very puzzling and you thought, "I don't know what to do about this. I don't know the answer to this"?

And maybe within a few minutes or sometimes within a few days, all of a sudden you think—at the most strange times, perhaps you're in the bath or you're driving along or you're hanging out your clothes or you're doing some working at your job—and all of a sudden into your mind comes the thought, "Oh, you know, if I did thus-and-so, that would solve the problem." You think, "Why didn't I think of that before? This is wonderful," and you have the answer. It is in that moment that you have touched into your sacred space, your higher self. And in that moment, your higher self is telling you...

You know, your higher self knows everything, literally and figuratively, everything. There is nothing that it doesn't know and as you need the information, it will give it to you. If you sit there and say, "I don't know what to do. Oh, I just don't know what to do. I don't know what to do." Every time you say, "I don't know what to do," you're building a blockage, a stone wall right here [draws] and you make it thicker and thicker and thicker and thicker and thicker.

But what happens if you say, "In this moment I appear not to know what to do. However, I know my divine self, my higher self, knows the answer so therefore I welcome whatever my divine self has to say to me." That divine self is sitting up there saying, "Yes! I've got the answer right here. Here we go," and it will give it to you.

Now, how does it give it to you? Sometimes through a voice in your own mind. Sometimes someone will say something to you and you'll think, "Oh, that's it! Of course." Sometimes you read it in a book, sometimes you read it in your newsprint, sometimes it will just be a quiet, gentle understanding that will come upon you, but I promise you, you will never be denied the answer that you seek from your higher self.

When you are helping others, you have to stay connected to your higher self because if you don't, you're not going to get truth, and if you're not giving out truth, then you are not teaching and you are not healing. You are fooling them and you're fooling yourself.

How many of you have gone to hear a lecture from someone and you realize as you listen that this person is speaking words that they don't believe in? You know it, don't you? You can feel that there is no foundation of truth or foundation of connectedness in what they're saying. They're saying it because they've read it somewhere or they've heard it and they know that's what you want to hear but they really don't have it inside.

Now, anyone can be an instrument of healing and get instant results if you are connected to your *truth* and if the person you're giving the healing to is willing to accept and take in the power that's there. Nothing is withheld from you, *ever,* of a spiritual nature. The moment you ask for it, it will be given to you because you have asked.

People think, "Oh, I'll ask but I'm not...I don't...it's just me so I don't think God's going to answer me, but I'll ask." So your prayer is, "Dear Father, I would like to be an instrument of healing for this person. I realize it's only me so You probably don't want to use me at all so therefore, I'm sorry to bother You. I hope I didn't interrupt Your lunch or something but if You could see to just do one little thing, just something, but if you can't, it's alright." (Laughter) What results are you going to get? None. Why? Because you are not coming from the truth of your being.

When the Master Jesus brought Lazarus out of the tomb—that wasn't the only person he raised from the dead but that's the one that is the most known so we'll use that for an example—when he walked up to the tomb, he pulled in his power. He just stood there for a moment and he felt that power. Then he contacted Lazarus and he said, "Lazarus, do you want to come back to the earth?" At first, Lazarus says, "Ah, I don't think so." (Laughter) Oh, he did. He said, "I don't think I want to." He said, "Well, make up your mind now, one way or the other." "Ah, I haven't finished what I started, have I?" "No, you didn't. You need to come back." (Laughter) "Well, okay." "Are you in agreement?" "Yes, I am in agreement. I shall come back." "All right." Then he said, the Master said, "Father, I thank You that You hear me for You hear me always." Always. He didn't say, "You hear me on Thursday, not on Saturday. You hear me now and then or if and when." He said, "You hear me always." And then he commanded Lazarus to come forth and Lazarus did.

It is with that same conviction that you pull in your power to heal or to teach, that same conviction. "Father, I thank You that You hear me for You hear me always," and then you heal. You don't let your ego get in there. Now, the ego is like this little wimpy servant. It goes about, *"Yes, yes, I shall help you. Yes, yes yes. Oh, don't go there. No, no, no. Oh, you better not do that. You'll fall flat on your face. Over here. See, there. Now you just sit here and be quiet and don't disturb anyone."* Do you want that? No.

When you heal you *heal* because you've got the power! You've got the power in your Spirit, in that sacred space within you, and all you need is to *do it!* It's *that* simple. "That isn't true," I see you all thinking. "That's easy for you to say. You're an angel. You should be down here and try that."

You are higher than angels. I've told you this before. We were created first, then God got this wondrous idea and He created you and He gave you free will. He gave you every power that He has. He gave you the potential to do anything you wanted. One of the things He gave you was creativity and imagination. All this works together in healing.

Then He said to us, "They're going out and they're going to create chaos and they're going to have a lot of fun playing and they're going to create all kinds of problems and they're going to get lost in them, so maybe you'd better toddle on with them and help. But He didn't say to us...oh, the other thing He said was, "Don't interfere with their free will. If they want to create chaos, let them play in it. Just keep them safe."

So, do you have the power to heal? Do you? Don't listen to the ego. The ego will pull you right out of contact with your Spirit Self and your sacred space. The ego wants you to believe that you can't do this because that's how it keeps control of you and that's not what you want.

How many of you in this past year of your time have faced a great challenge in your life? I don't mean necessarily an earth-shattering life or death thing but just a great challenge that really required of you to make a commitment to yourself and to something else. How long did you belabor yourselves over that? How many fires of hell did you walk through of your own making before you came to your own conclusions? Quite a few. Some of them were pretty hot, weren't they? (Laughter) Couldn't sleep...wake up in the middle of the night thinking about it. Couldn't eat or else couldn't stop eating. Got all out of sorts with friends and relatives. Didn't feel you could handle it. Wanted to run away. Wished you had never begun it. Ahh...thought of getting a new job, a new husband, new wife, new something, anything, but let-me-out-of-here type of thinking?

But when you once made the commitment, what happened? Peace and a shift in energy, eh? Did it not seem to you that all of the things that seemed impossible before became possibilities? Didn't you notice that the fear that you had before kind of went away?

Now, it's that kind of commitment that you have to have if you're going to be a healer/teacher. That is never a part-time, sometime, when-I-feel-like-it job. When you have said, "I want to heal or I want to teach,"—they're the same thing—you have to make a commitment that you are going to do the very best that you know how to do and you are not going to listen to the ego self of you that's going to throw every fear in the world in your face and say, "Here, deal with that one!" You're going to say, "I am a child of God. I am *Spirit in form* and I will live my life from the Spirit of me, which is the God Self of me. Everything I chose to do, I do with power."

Now, whether you realize it or not, you've done all your failures with power. That's why you were so successful at failing. You always use power even when you *think* you are not using power. That's what makes things happen. However, when you *consciously* touch in to your higher self and you work from *that* point, then you are in your sacred space and everything you do has to come out right. It *has* to. That is the law. God is in command and you are God's child and you are in command of yourself and anything you set your Spiritual Self to do, *you can do* and nothing can stop you excepting yourself when you begin to fear or doubt.

When you are doing a healing, it is very important that the person you are doing the healing on recognizes that you are the instrument...that *they* are the ones who are responsible for healing themselves because that is a grand truth. Even the Master Jesus didn't heal everyone he touched. If he touched someone and they didn't want to be healed, they were not healed.

There was a situation in which a daughter brought her aged and ailing father to the Master and she said, "I love my father dearly. I can't bear to see him like this. Would you please restore him to himself?" And Jesus went to his higher self and he said to the man, "What do you want me to do?" And the man said to him, "I have lived many years. I am weary of the earth. I desire greatly to leave. I ask that you grant me a peaceful death."

And Jesus said, "Your daughter wants you to remain." He said, "No, I cannot remain for her. I cannot remain for anyone but myself and I do not care to stay." And so the Master said, "Then so be it," and the man passed peacefully away within a few minutes. And the daughter was greatly distressed. She spat upon Jesus and cursed him and she called him all manner of foul names, wept over her father, and saw no God act in anything that happened.

You know, that could happen to you. What would you do if you were called to a hospital to give someone healing and they died while your hands were on them? Did you ever think of that? What would you do? Would you say, "I'm never going to touch anyone again. I do and they're dead as a doornail"? No. You would know that the energy and the love that you brought to them allowed them to do exactly what they wanted, to leave their body, and what you gave them was the gift of peaceful passing.

Now, some of you here will have that experience. You will be in the midst of a healing and the person will pass away. Oh, not at Fellowships in the chair, no. (Laughter) Aren't you glad for that? Indeed. But as you go forth into the world to do these things, you have to be willing to accept the outcome and know that what you gave from your heart was indeed a wondrous gift, no matter how the person chose to use it. Doesn't matter. The gift was sacred and holy and used just as it had been intended.

A lot of people don't realize that death is a kind of healing. They always think that healing means the person gets better and gets up and goes about. Many times, a person needs there to be a healer there in order for them to leave. They need that little extra energy to use, to take the step.

Most everyone, no matter what their beliefs are, are afraid to die because there's always that little glimmer at the last moment of, "What if all I've learned isn't so? What happens if when I leave this body, there is nothing of me? What if there is nothing after death?" That happens to everyone. For just that little flickering second, there is the element of doubt, and sometimes the presence of a healer is the only thing that keeps that doubt at bay...is just the power that you are bringing in.

Healing in the World

Everyone's afraid to be healed. You don't think so? Why do you think people hang on to their illnesses even though they have been to the doctors and they are on medication and they have gone to all the healing centers and have all the healers working on them and they still don't heal? Why do you think that be?

It is because they are fearful of perfect health. If they have perfect health, look at all of the responsibilities that could come their way. Look at all the things they would have to do. They would have to give up being waited upon and being prayed over and all that sort of thing, so a lot of people really, really don't want to be healed.

What do you do then? You've got all this power. You counsel with their higher self and you give energy to them to use *as they choose* and if they use it to leave the earth, that is their choice.

You never force your will upon another. A lot of healers think they have to *will* the person well because if the person doesn't get well, that's a reflection upon the healer. No, it isn't. You came and did what you were asked to do and what they do with it is their choice. You don't ever force your will upon another. You don't ever say, "I'm going to heal you even if you don't *want* to be healed." You wouldn't want someone to do that to you. And healing is done with love, and don't ever forget that.

I want you to close your eyes and we're going to do three oms.

Om... Om... Om...

[Gabriel leads a guided meditation.]

Put yourself inside an elevator. The door closes and you feel yourself going up. As you go up, you feel a lightness in your being. It's as though everything of the earth is falling away and you are becoming lighter and lighter. You feel every concern that you have ever had fall away from your mind, every emotional disturbance is gone from your emotional body.

You are becoming light, becoming light, becoming light, and you realize that you are light and that light fills the inside of the elevator. You feel the elevator stop, the doors open, and you step out into the vastness of forever. Around about you is every conceivable scene of beauty and light and you are a part of that light.

You feel yourself going forward. Before you there stands a figure—glorious, radiant figure—and as you approach, it holds out its arms to you for an embrace, and it embraces you and as you look up into its face, you see yourself. The radiance and the power of it seems to wrap around you and you recognize that you are one with it.

And as you are enfolded in its embrace, you feel yourself becoming consumed in it, a part of it, until there is nothing that separates the two of you. You have become one. You feel that oneness. You sense it in every part of your being.

You feel yourself being drawn back to the elevator. You and your Spirit Self remain unified together. You step into the elevator, the doors close, and you are still in this great and wondrous light, and you feel the elevator going down but the light does not diminish. Downward... The light still bright and pulsating. Downward... The light still bright, still filling your being. The elevator stops and you step off and you are this beauteous light being. You come over and you sit back down in your seat, still radiant light.

When I count to three, you will open your eyes, still being radiant light. One. Two. Three.

My how bright you are! Is there anyone here who didn't feel themselves becoming light? That, beloveds, is how you connect to your God Self. It's as simple as going upward, meeting that God Self, and recognizing the At-one-ment between you.

I want you to do this every day. It would be good if you did it upon arising in the morn and sometime through your evening hour before you get sleepy and noddy. Just do that exercise until after a bit, you won't need the elevator. You will simply close your eyes and you'll feel yourself going up and making that connection.

Now, before you do healing, you should do this. You should go up to your higher self, make that connection, and come back as your higher self because that is when you will begin to experience your sacred space, the field of energy that is around you. You will begin to feel it. Some of you may even see it. Then you will do your healing.

It only takes a moment. The more you do it, the more rapidly it comes to you 'til after a bit, you can simply close your eyes and you're there.

Now, when you do this, you will find that your healing begins to take on a new kind of energy. People will begin to notice and say, "You know, you've done healings before on me but this was different. I could feel something different." And they will recognize. They may not know how to say what it is. They may not say, "Well, I think your higher self was here," (laughter) but they will feel the power.

Supposing you're in a situation... Some of you have relatives and close friends who think you're a little daft to be in this work so you can't say to them, "Excuse me, I'm going to my higher self. Be back in five minutes." (Laughter) But what you can do... Let us suppose you're in a situation where healing is needed but you are not free to say that you're going to do this. By getting yourself acquainted with this method and using it, you'll find that all you have to do is close your eyes for just a second and you can *be* there. Then you can do it without anyone knowing what's going on. You can be in a room with someone who would totally discount healing and give them a healing and they won't even know what's happening.

A few years ago, Beloved Woman's relative, her brother...he has a little doggie—a little poodle, very delicate little doggie—and the little doggie fell off of something, the couch I guess it was, and when he landed, he landed on his head and neck and he twisted around and he went out. He became unconscious and he was in this twisted position.

And they called Beloved Woman and...what is the doggie's name? Shanny. And they called Beloved Woman and she said, "Well, bring him down." Well, the wife was quite distraught and very much in tears, "Oh, poor little thing. I do believe he is dead," and so on and so forth. And Beloved Woman sent her out of the room and she had only her brother stay because he was much more calm. And she put him on the floor and she knelt down by him and she put her hands upon him and she went to her higher self and she said to him, "Shanny, what do you want? Do you want to come back to the earth or do you want to leave?"

And he wanted to stay so she put her hands on him and she said, "Father, Thou art the life in this little creature and I ask that this life be restored." And then she said to the doggie, "Shanny, you are healed," and straight away the glaze left his eyes, he turned his head, and her brother who was sitting on the floor in front of him...the little doggie looked up at her and then looked around, stood up, and she said, "Go to Daddy," and he ran over and he scrambled up into a most grateful Daddy's lap and Daddy grabbed him up and hugged him.

And to this day—now, this happened two or three years ago—to this day when she goes to visit, before she even gets the door open, that little doggie knows it is her and he's dancing all about at the door and when she comes in, there's nothing will do but she picks him up and he just melts right into her.

And he's not a doggie that goes readily to others but the healing that she gave him touched into him in such a way he will never forget it as long as he lives. No matter how great a length of time might pass that they do not see each other, he will remember her because of that energy, that life that came back to him because of what she did.

Now, when you do a healing, you are affecting that person's earth life for as long as they are upon the earth, even if you never see them again. On a higher level there is a connectedness between you that remains. Sometimes it will remain for many lifetimes—not diminishing, not stopping because of laying aside physical bodies and coming back again or anything. Nothing diminishes that connectedness. And it is a connectedness that is of the Spirit and it is a very sacred holy connectedness.

Now, this does not *bind* you to them. There is nothing binding about healing at all. It is a free-flowing, generous vibration. But there is a connectedness and even if years should pass and that person comes back into your life, even if only in a casual way, they will not ever forget you. They will remember that connection and you will remember it too. You might not remember them particularly but you will know when you are near them. There is a feeling. There is a feeling there.

Now, what is that? That is the unification of the truth of your beings. Now remember, you all came forth from God. All at the same time you were breathed forth and in a sense you are siblings. In a very pure sense you are all *one*. You are individualized units of that one single breathing forth of being.

And when you do healing—true, true healing from the very God Self of you—what you are doing is you are reconnecting to that feeling that was between you when you first were breathed forth into beingness. At that point, you looked at each other with great joy. It was like you just discovered something wondrous and there was a lot of embracing and a lot of touching as though to touch another was to make valid your own sense of is-ness. And there was such love, such unconditional love. You loved each other intensely with great devotion, great tenderness, great joy, and healing done from the Spirit of you re-establishes that connectedness and there is that welcome home-ness kind of feeling that comes between the healer and the healee. Doesn't matter who does which. From the Spirit there is that coming together, that At-one-ment once more.

If someone were to say to you, "Oh, I am greatly distressed. Can you give me a reading?" You would simply, of course, sit down and do it, wouldn't you? Would you be afraid that what you said to them might not be so? Would you? You would? Why? You don't know? Your ego getting in the way, indeed.

The same thing happens with the healing part. So there is one thing that you all have to develop and that is *trust*. Now, who are you not trusting? You're not trusting yourselves. You think that between you and your higher self there is a little person called Judas who is going to betray you. "What if I ask for this and I don't get it?"

I shall tell you a grand truth. You are never denied anything you ask in a spiritual way. When you ask to be a healer, before you've got the whole sentence out of your thought process, you are granted that.

[Someone sneezes.] God bless you. May your higher self bless your lower self. (Laughter) Where do you think the sneeze came from, the higher self or the lower self? I've never heard a higher self sneeze. (Laughter)

When you ask to help another in *any* way—whether it be healing, counseling, reading, whatever, doesn't matter—it is granted and you must never doubt that, ever. You must never doubt that.

When I first came to Beloved Woman back before she was afraid to let the world know I was Gabriel, she was so full of fears back then. "What will people think? They will think I am crazy. Blah, blah, blah." Who cares?

Anyway, she used to...before we would do a seminar she would worry. First it was, "What if he doesn't show up?" (Laughter) That was always the first one. "What if I get there and he doesn't come?" Well, after a bit, she realized I wasn't going to do that to her, *then*. Then she thought, "What's going to come out of my mouth? What if he says this or says that? What if what he says people don't like? What if?" And we went through that scenario with her.

Well, after a bit, she'd come to realize that what came out of my mouth was a truth and that nobody was after her hide or anything of the sort for it. So she learned to trust that I would always be there and she learned to trust that what I taught was so. She had come to a complete trust in me in every sense of the word. After a bit, she never wondered what I was going to talk about or anything of the sort...never bothered about it, never gave it another thought.

Now, she has before her a time of teaching as herself *from* her higher self. That's coming up very shortly. I only have a little over a year and then I am gone. Then The One [the Master Jesus] will come for a bit and then little by little it is going to be just her. When I say just her, I mean her higher self.

Now, we've talked to her about this and it was the same scenario. "What if I can't do it? What's going to happen if I try to go to my higher self and my higher self has moved?" (Laughter) "Then, how will I know what to say? What shall I do?"

And I thought, "We've got to get her over this." So, there was a group of psychiatrists and psychologists and people who deal with the mentally ill who requested a counsel session with me. They asked me if I would come and teach them how the mind works. And Beloved Woman asked me, "Would I do this?" and I said, "Tell them to gather. A teacher will be there." Now, she immediately assumed it would be me and I let her assume it. And about three hours before the meeting I came to her and I said, "Beloved Woman, I am not going to be there tonight."

Now, these are people who traveled—some up from New York City, some from California, some...they came from all over the United States—and she looked at me and said, "You're, you're, you're joking." I said, "No, Beloved Woman. I am not going to be there." "Well, who's going to be there?" she said. I said, "*You* are going to be there." "Oh, oh...well...now." I said, "Now, you listen." I said, "You are going to go there and you are going to teach them." "*I* am going to teach...? They have degrees in this and degrees in that and what not." I said, "Beloved Woman, be at peace."

So she called the facilitator and she said to him, "Gabriel isn't coming tonight," and he thought, "Oh, my God," and I said, "That's exactly right." So he took a deep breath and he said, "What shall we do?" She said, "I'll come." He said, "Okay, we'll go with that."

So when they got there, there was about twenty-five, I guess, of them there. She said to him, because they met at his place, she said, "Have you told them?" He said, "Oh, no." (Laughter) He said, "*You're* going to tell them."

Now, these were people who were strangers to her. These were people who had never witnessed channeling. There were probably, out of the group, maybe five who had ever witnessed channeling and the rest of them it was all just some kind of a strange phenomena.

So the facilitator introduced her and said, "I turn the whole thing over to you." (Laughter) Now, while he was talking to them, she prayed, "Dear Father, be Thou the words I speak. Be Thou the truth I give. Let nothing come from me that is not truth." So she stood up and she said, "Gabriel isn't coming," and they're all looking like...looking at each other. Now some of these people had flown in from quite a distance away. She said, "However, if you want your money back and you want to leave, you can." But she said, "*I* will teach you what has been taught to me," and she said, "If none of you want to stay, I will understand." No one left, no one.

She took a deep breath, she went to her higher self, and she taught non-stop for two hours. Now, these are people who are trained about the mind—psychiatrists and psychologists, professors of that. She taught for two hours and when it was over, she got a standing ovation. They all came up, delighted they had come, learned a lot. Several of them said that she had answered questions that they had had in their mind for years and had researched and had never been able to find the answers to.

And after they all left, she burst into tears. (Laughter) And going home, she said to me... I said to her, "Well, Beloved Woman, I see you did well." "Don't ever do that to me again," she said. (Laughter) I said, "Oh, you ain't seen nothing yet." (Laughter)

Now, I did not say that to her to be mean, but I did it to prove something to her and what is true of her is true of you. Your higher self, your God Self, can do anything. *Anything*. And if she could stand there and teach learned people about their own profession and have them learn and listen and absorb and be delighted with what she said, then any of you can do anything like that and more.

The Master Jesus said, "These things that I do, ye shall do and greater things yet than these." And he wasn't just being polite. He was speaking a grand truth. And why is that a truth? Because the same Spirit that was in him, the same child of Godness that was in him, is in you, because at the moment that you were breathed forth, he was breathed forth *with* you and you are all the same.

When you are healing, *remember who you are.* And I'm not talking about the names that you have now or the bodies that you occupy. I'm talking about the God Self of you because that is where your power is and that is the power that you use.

There is a great difference in the ego saying [robotically], "I can do that," and in the God Self of you saying [softly], "I can do that." The ego speaks from error perception. There is nothing underneath, no foundation beneath the ego's words. They are like feathers on the wind. But the God Self of you is the truth of your being and it will never, ever, ever fail you under any circumstance. Anything that you need to know or to do is available to you if you will accept it.

But most people think, "Oh, I couldn't do that. That's too egotistical. Who am I to think that I could heal? Oh, who am I to think that I could do this or do that?" And the ego gets in the way and convinces you that you can't, and that's why when I asked you if someone asked you for a reading, would you worry if what you said was so and this entity said, "Yes." That's the ego of you telling you, "What if you're wrong?" How can God be wrong? How can anything that is coming from the truth of your being not be true? It's impossible. That's like turning on your water faucet and expecting to get coffee or something else. It's not going to happen.

Healing in the World

When you tune in to your Source, when you are up here in your Spirit Self, that is exactly what you're going to get and you're not going to get anything lesser than that.

As Beloved Woman said, "Let the words that I speak be truth. Let only truth come through me." When you do healing, "Let the energy that comes through me be pure and holy...[inaudible]...or never fail to give a true, good healing."

You are not doing this to prove to the world that you're famous or you're wonderful or you're going to be the talk of the town, are you? Because if you are, you're coming from your ego and you will fail. But if you are doing it because you truly want to help...every single one of you truly wants to help. There are no egotistical people in here. Well, some of you have a little ego but nothing you can't boot in the pants and get rid of. (Laughter)

But when you come from your true self and your desire is *only* to help—and it doesn't matter whether people remember it was you or not, as long as they get the results—then you can know that you will *never* fail. How could you fail? You can't.

You will bring truth and the people you bring it to will use it how they will but the fact remains, you are bringing truth and that is what matters. Anything less than that and you'd be better off to do something else. If you can't be true, then don't do it. There are many charlatans in your field of work. Many people who are in it for the honor and the glory. And that's all they will get, earthly honor and earthy glory, and when it is over, what will they have? Nothing.

But when you are coming from your heart, from the true part of you, then what you give is lasting. It is eternal. Your gift is very pure. Giving from the ego is an empty gift and it will benefit no one, especially you. But the truth of your being never fails you. Never.

I would like to have you do some practice healings on one another. Okay, I want you to partner up with someone because we're going to have you do healings and then we're going to have you be healed. And I want you to go...as you're doing your healing, I want you to go to your higher self, go within. I'm not going to talk you through it. I've given you the method. Now you can use it. I want you to go to your higher self and then follow the guidance of your higher self. Do the healing however you feel led from within you to do, or follow how you were taught at your school. Doesn't matter, but let it come from the within of you. The only preconceived idea I want you to hold in your mind is that the person you are giving the healing to *is in perfect health*.

Those of you who are being healed, I want you to leave yourselves open like a great sponge. I don't want you to have any preconceived ideas of what you should feel or if you should see anything or anything of that kind. Your purpose is to be healed and that is your only purpose. Visions or feelings or anything...those are all side things. If they come, good. If they don't come, good. But your purpose in being healed is just that, to be healed.

Let the healing happen on whatever level you need it. Some of you might need it physically, some of you emotionally, some of you have a turmoil in your mind about something. Some of you are just dealing with basic fear. But leave yourself open to receive the healing in whatever area is the greatest need, and just sit there and receive.

Then after you do that, we're going to switch around. I'd like you to switch partners and then the healers become the healees. And I want you to see for yourselves how *you* feel when you are doing the healing, when you are connected to your higher self. Now, do you have any questions about this at all? Then choose a partner and go for it! (Laughter)

[Participants practice healing each other.]

All of you got to your higher self. Some of you had a little problem staying there, holding onto it, but you did get to the higher self. Now, I noticed that some of you, when you really begin to get into the healing, seem to lose the connection between your self and your higher self, and you seemed more preoccupied with *method*, of what you were to do next and so forth.

You followed your regime, which is all right, but the important thing is to stay...to keep that connectedness. Now, some of you did pretty well but none of you held it all the way through, lthough a lot of you held it for a very long time.

You in the back there...I don't know names...the middle. You did very well holding the connection until you hit a certain part with the person you were working with and then you began to concentrate on that and you lost your connectedness, but you did very well.

You did very well with your connectedness. You really got into the healing part of it but then you had trouble keeping your focus. Your mind kept getting away from you and you'd haul it back. That's all right. Now, you'll encounter that.

You and your partner did well excepting that you had a problem with your focus too. Your mind drifted. You had to keep pulling your thoughts back.

And you had the same problem. You did a little better with the focus until just near the end and then your mind went totally off. (Laughter)

You did a little better with the focus but you didn't have a good connectedness. You'd remember it and you'd go back and then you'd get off and then you'd go back and you'd ...

Now, the reason I'm pointing these things out to you is because none of that is wrong. I don't want you to think, "Oh, I did wrong," or "I did badly." What it is showing you is the areas in which you need to work at. Now, practice makes perfect with this and after a bit, as you practice...

Now you, you did very well with the receiving part. You did excellent with your receiving part.

You kept concerning yourself whether you are doing it right.

Now, you did very good on receiving too and you also...the two of you did a similar thing. You had a little problem with what comes next. "Am I doing this right? Yes, okay, I know where I am now." And you kind of had it.

Now, these things happen but it's all right. When they happen, all you have to do is recognize they're happening and just gently but firmly bring your concentration back to the higher self first and then to the healing. Always make your connection with the higher self.

You get concerned about what you are or are not seeing. Forget it. It doesn't matter what you're seeing.

Beloved entity, you did very well with both the receiving and the giving. You were very concentrated. You began to lose touch a little with your higher self toward the end of giving the healing. You became concerned about the person you were working with whether or not he was comfortable and you got a little off track there.

But most of you, considering all things, I thought you did excellent. You really did very, very well.

You did very well in the receiving part. You were very open and taking it in very nicely, very nicely. You get a little too worried in the healing part but when you were concentrated, your healing was very powerful. You just had a little trouble with your concentration.

Now, the thing is... Did any of you feel a shift in energy with this method of going to your higher self?

Participants: Yes.

Gabriel: You did feel a difference? Now, in the receiving part, did you feel any differences? What were they?

Participant: Pressure in my temples and crown chakra.

Gabriel: Anyone else?

Participant: I kind of had shudders and I couldn't breathe for a second.

Participant: A lightness.

Participant: I felt a lightness and a [inaudible] inside, almost like if somebody had a physical cleansing or a physical colonic. It was like an energy...an energetic...it was real clear inside. It was real different.

Gabriel: And you felt a lightness? The energy that you bring in from your higher self is very pure. It's a very pure, pure energy. So, feelings of lightness, temples, in the throat chakra, especially when you're doing the healing, you should feel...I shouldn't say, "You should." Some of you will. Some of you won't. Some of you never will and that's all right. That doesn't mean it isn't working.

But in the throat chakra, when you are doing the healing...cause this is a new...this idea of using *your power* is kind of new to you. You've heard it, you've been taught it, and you think, "Yes, I can do that," and then when you get up there to do it, you think, "Maybe I'd better not use *too* much power," so you pull back on it.

Now, when you were sitting opposite each other, it was interesting to me that the flow of energy between the two of you did not change no matter which of you was healing or which of you was receiving. Did you notice the sameness? It remained the same. There was an even exchange going on all the time. I thought that was rather interesting because it was a little hard to tell who was doing what. (Laughter)

Beloveds, there is no wrong way to heal. Everyone has their own method, their own procedure, and any procedure you use is correct if that is your belief system. So don't feel that one method is better than another method. Whatever method puts you in tune with that higher self and is allowing you to bring that pure energy through. Whatever the method, use it. If it works for you, use it.

How many of you work with instruments such as burning incense or perfumes or candles or using herbs? You can direct your energy into the essences you use and work that way if you are more comfortable with it. If you feel that you would rather not be the main focus, you can pour your energy into your candles or into your perfumes or whatever and let it defuse out to the person in that method if you are more comfortable doing that. Some people would rather direct the attention away from themselves and work that way and there's nothing wrong with that.

How many of you use herbs? Same thing. Put your energies into the herbs. Any method that you can use that will conduct the energy to the person is perfectly acceptable. Some of you might use gemstones, the placing of crystals here or there on the body. Same thing. Put the energy into the stone.

Now, the most direct method is from you to them but any method that makes you relax and be comfortable so that you're not *concerned* about yourself. "Am I doing it right? Am I standing too close? Am I too far away? Oh, I lost my concentration. Now what will I do? I'll start it all over again." Whatever takes your mind off of *you* and the method, whatever brings you into that clear desire for healing to work, use it because there is *no wrong way to heal.*

Keep your centeredness on your highest self, on the God-power working through you. Keep your centeredness on the person receiving it. Never put energy into the ailment. Never think, "Oh, this person has cancer. This person has this, that, or something else," because then you're feeding energy into the ailment. You don't want that. *Always envision perfection. Always.*

Now, have any of you anything to ask of me before you take your food break?

Participant: One day after reading a story about Jesus doing healing in the Bible to my son, he said to me, "Mommy, so many healers that we know touch people and Jesus spoke the Word. Why don't people today speak the Word and what's the Word, Mommy?" (Laughter) So I'm asking you, Gabriel, how do you answer that?

Gabriel: What's the Word? The word he spoke was Aramaic, which I will not attempt to put her tongue through because she doesn't have the facility to get the guttural sounds out. However, speaking the Word simply means a proclamation of that which you desire. In other words, what the Master was saying was, "In the name and through the power of the living God, be thou whole as thou was created." And that is the "word."

And why don't people speak the Word? Because they think they can't. They think they don't know the Word and they also don't think that those kinds of things are possible this day upon your earth.

I tell you great truth... More people are healed through prayer than are healed through medicine, and this is not casting aspersions upon medicine, for God heals through medicine too, but a sincere prayer from the heart has more power than people have any idea of. When you truly desire to be an instrument of healing, indeed *you are that*. You are that and nothing can take it away from you. Any other questions?

Participant: You say, "Picture perfection." How do you picture perfection?

Gabriel: You picture...if you are working with a physical ailment, you picture the body with *no* physical ailment in *perfect* health. What does perfect health look like? It looks like a body that is functioning in every way to its full capacity.

After your food break, we're going to talk a little bit about specific illnesses and what their causes be and how to work with cause because working with cause is just as powerful—more powerful, in a way—than working with the effect.

***

Causes of Ailments

Fear is a dark force. It is a false force. It has no basis of truth in it. There is no Spirit in fear. Fear is a product completely, totally, of the ego. It mixes in with the personality and the two join forces, as it were, to manifest blockages, adverse conditions in your life. Now, it depends upon too in what direction the fear is pointed, so to say, as to what it produces. It can produce anything from a mild headache to the total inability for one to move out of a chair. Perhaps its most insidious out-picturing is that of illness in the physical body because every illness is based upon fear of some kind.

Now, your body in its out-picturing is a reflection of the various states of spiritual understanding. Every part of your body has a counterpart in spirit that is not a body but rather a belief system so when an ailment attacks a certain portion of the body, you can go to a belief system and you can trace it back, and it is that that you should seek to heal, for without healing the cause, the effectual healings will only be temporary.

Have you not heard of people who received a healing, seemed to be quite well indeed, and then several weeks or months later the ailment reestablished itself in the body? And one wonders what happened then. What happened is that the body received the healing but the cause of the ailment was never addressed. So therefore, the cause just reproduced the same symptoms in the body all over again.

I have studied with Rembrandt, as you shall see shortly here. (Laughter) [Gabriel draws another figure.] Well, after some consideration, I think that's more Picasso. What think you? (Laughter) How's that? Shall we give him a bit of hair? There.

Now, you have the structure of your body, which is, of course, your **skeleton**. Now, without a skeleton in it, the body would not be able to stand upright. It would not be able to even sit up or do anything but slither along the ground actually. So the bone structure of the body represents your basic concept of your Spirit Self. In other words, it represents what you *think* you are.

The **head**, your **skull** as it were, being encasing your **brain**, represents a kind of protection of ideas. In other words, it represents the concept that what is inside your head belongs only to you. No one else can get inside your head and find out what's there. So, it is a kind of a privacy that would, by human consciousness, would represent that aspect of you that nothing external can touch. So you have here up in the skull [draws], you have the basis of your individual part of you that can never be violated. In other words, no one can get inside your head. So this would represent your very private self.

Now, people are interesting when it comes to their private thoughts. It's one of the few things that people aren't willing to share. It represents that part of you that is known only to God because truly no one can know your thoughts excepting you willingly disclose them. Even if someone were to read your mind, as you call it, which is not totally possible unless you are extremely evolved, even if they perchance hit upon a thought that you've had and they say to you, "You were thinking thus-and-so, weren't you?" and you would think, "Well, yes, I was," you still have the option of denying it. You can still say, "Well no, I wasn't actually thinking that at all." So, there still remains this privacy that cannot be violated.

So, when something goes wrong in the brain—such as a tumor, a growth of some sort, or as occasionally happens, some part of the brain is missing in a fetus when it is developing—that always represents that whether it be from a past life, which it mostly always is, that this individual has the concept that even their own thoughts are not theirs, that somehow, somewhere they have been violated when it comes to their internal thinking.

Now, perhaps as a child they had a parent or a teacher in school—sometimes teachers do this not realizing—who insist that the child tell them everything. Now, a lot of moms and dads do this only with the intent of protecting the child so they would say to the little one, "Now tell Mommy or Daddy what you are thinking. What were you thinking when aunt so-and-so said this or that to you?" Or "What were you thinking when you did this or that?" In other words, the parent is pulling out of the child the privacy that the child feels is their very own and they are being denied that. Or a parent who goes into the child's room and looks through all their belongings in the absence of the child. This happens to teenagers a lot. Anything that would make that individual feel that what is between them and God, which is sacred to them, has been violated, somewhere, somehow. That will produce tumors in the brain, cancer of the brain. Anything that is an invasion of that space, whether it be viral or bacterial or whatever it is that invades that space, is an out-picturing of this person's idea that they have nothing that is *totally only* their own. Now, this may not be a conscious...very rarely is a conscious thought or a conscious memory but it always produces a problem in the head.

Now, we're not going to get into insanity and all that because that's a mental thing. I want to talk about the physical body here.

Now, in your bone structure, all of the bones depend upon your **spine**, for the bony part of your spine is the guardian of your **spinal cord** and that is a very delicate thing and if it is injured at any point produces paralysis. So, the bony structure of your spine, of your neck bones and your spine, is extremely important in the well being of the physical body, and injury from the shoulders up in through the neck...

Now in the **neck** right here is the **throat** chakra and here is where your power center is. Whenever you have a problem with your power, whenever you are questioning your power or whether or not you should use your power, or whether or not you have any power, you will usually manifest a **sore throat**, a cold in the throat, or if it is a chronic feeling that your power is not your own, it can develop into any kind of malady: malfunction of the glands in the neck, of the **thymus** and the **thyroid**, and so forth. Because the power center is the place from which your actions come, it is when you feel in your power that you will take an action of some kind, and procrastination often affects people adversely in the throat area. Know you people who will always put off until tomorrow anything that they can get away with not doing today? And failure to act, unwillingness to go forward, often produces a chronic condition in the throat, which can develop into **throat cancer**, in its extreme, or right on down to a simple cold in the throat. **Laryngitis** always reflects one's unwillingness to speak up, whether it be on their behalf or on behalf of their belief system or of another.

Now, in the **bones of the neck**, which I want to differentiate here from the glands...these support the head. Even if you have a fine spine, if your neck bones are absent, your head is going to flop about and you are not going to be able to hold your head up.

So a problem in the neck area always represents the fear that there is no support for their privacy, no support for their internal ideas, no support for their thought system. In other words, they feel they are isolated. There is nothing to support their thinking process.

A lot of people sustain a neck injury in automobile accidents. What do you call it? **Whiplash**. And that usually is a manifestation of that person's feeling that, in effect, their ideas or their thinking is not supported by those around them. So consequently, they have these...you see people going around holding their necks. What they need to do is to establish that they are their own support. God supports them and they don't need the support of other people.

Now, as you get into the **shoulder area** you have bones across here. I don't know all the terms of your bones. Is that clavicle? **Clavicle**, all right. Now, this gives support to the muscles that hold your arms, give you the ability to move your arms, so these are very important muscles, very important bones across here. And the person who breaks...what do you call your sleeve bone? No. Collarbone. A person who sustains injury to a collarbone usually feels overburdened. They don't...they can't raise their arms. They can't use their muscles, the upper torso, because they aren't able, they aren't smart enough, they aren't rich enough, they aren't whatever enough, educated enough. You pick it and they can find that they are not enough of it and they will frequently sustain injuries or even ailments that affect that...**arthritis** up in this area.

Now, you also have your **rib cage** and your...not breast plate...**sternum**. Now, these give the ribs something to hang onto from the spine round the back and so forth. They also protect all of your **lungs**, your **heart**. Now, if the lungs and heart are not protected, death could ensue even if you just bumped yourself a little bit in the chest. If you were to fall down hard as children do when they ride down on the snow on their sleds, dashing themselves down onto it, if they had not the rib cage and the sternum bone to protect it, it would cause their death because the heart would be jiggled. You could also get a lung punctured simply by someone elbowing you in a crowd. You could have all manner of fatal injury if it were not for the ribs. So the ribs are a kind of a protection *around your life*. And when one feels that that protection is missing or in danger or in some way violated, they frequently will sustain injury or an ailment to the rib bones.

There are people, women mostly—oh, I'm not going to offend anyone...no, no, no (laughter)—who for cosmetic reasons have the last ribs removed so that they can have a tinier middle. They find in doing so that as they age they have difficulties in breathing. They develop tenderness all through that area. Why? Because the organs that are contained in there are not meant to be exposed and their tiny little middles do not make up for the problems they come into later on.

Now, the ribs also represent your sense of security. How secure do you feel in your world? Do you feel that your whole life system is in mortal danger? And some people do. It's not a conscious feeling. I don't mean you expect to walk out in the street and have someone mug you or something. I'm talking about your ability, your right, to live as you choose. Now, when someone feels that they don't have that right or that there are others who are forcing their will upon them, they will very often develop ailments in through the chest area that most always has to do with the spine.

Now remember, all of your ribs are attached in the back to your spine and these little bones in the back have little holes through them through which your **nervous system**... We'll make your nervous system the color of lilacs. [Draws] How is that? That's not the color of lilacs? Violets. All right, have it your way.

Now, out from your...let's make the spine this color too [draws]...out from your spine you have all these little nerves that go out to the various parts of the body and they see to it that your body gets energy to various parts. Every single organ in your body has a corresponding... What do you call them? Nerves? And they branch out and they have little fingers and so on and so forth that reach into various... So if you've a problem with your liver, it could come from the fact that that vertebrae that supplies energy to that organ has been blocked off. You have a **misalignment**...is that your term? Now, all of that would produce a problem with the liver. If you get your bones put back in place, a lot of times your liver will start to function again. Is that not so?

So, the **spine** not only supports the whole body, it also is the source through which every organ in your body receives energy, which is in turn, life. So this is a very important mechanism. A **spinal injury** anywhere along the spine can result in malfunctioning of organs or, in its worse case, **paralysis** of some part of the body. So, the spine would represent everything that you *uphold* in your belief system, everything that is important to you, everything that is the very basis and criteria of how you live your life.

Injury to the **lower part of the spine** that would affect the **legs** and **lower viscera** would represent a person who feels that they have no support from family. There is no one going to stand behind them, as it were. There is no one going to stand with them or be in accordance with them.

Anyone who has a problem through the **middle part**, which would affect the **stomach**, **pancreas**, and so forth, that would be someone who felt fear as far as ability to take in and digest new things and ideas. Your stomach always represents your ability to digest new information. So, if you've got tummy troubles, the basis for those tummy troubles is usually because you feel that you're not smart enough. "I don't know what they're talking about so how am I going to understand or digest this information?"

This also holds true of the **upper intestine**. The feeling that you cannot learn. Perhaps you've been told as a child...little girls used to be told this frequently, "Oh, you're not going to be good in mathematics because only boys are good in mathematics. Girls don't have the brains for mathematics." So a lot of women who *do* have the brains for mathematics also have stomach trouble and upper intestinal problems because they feel they're in a territory where they should not be.

Up in here in the spine has to do with the **heart**, the **lungs**, the **esophagus**, and also the **sternum** works in conjunction with the spine in the back here to produce a protection for these organs, as I said. But if there is the feeling there is no financial stability in the family or that they are the only financially responsible person, they will develop difficulty in the sternum, in between the **shoulder blades**, and in breathing.

A person who is the sole support of a family who is very ungrateful or who appears to be ungrateful very frequently develops **breathing problems— bronchitis, asthma, emphysema**—anything that would make it difficult to take in air. Why? Because they feel, number one, it isn't going to matter how much air they take in, they don't have the right to breathe because they are responsible for everybody all around them.

How many of you here have breathing problems from time to time? Are you or were you made responsible financially for debts, perhaps, that were not your own? Did you feel at one time that if you didn't work, everyone around you would starve, including yourself? Did you feel, perhaps, that you didn't have the right to take in life? Yes, you did. (Laughter)

All of this goes to the **spine**, which is the support of the body and represents the support of your life.

Now, your **arms** and your **hands** serve so many purposes. Your hands represent your ability to reach out and to receive, your ability to grasp and to hang onto. Hands can heal and hands can kill. A person can take their hand and lay it upon another and bring healing. A person can take their hand and squeeze the life out of another person.

So hands represent how you express your inner self. Some people's hands are warm and gentle; other people's hands are cold and cruel. It represents your use of your power. If you notice, the power center is in direct alignment with your arm.

People who have trouble with their arms, or especially their hands, feel that either they are not able to utilize what they know or they have, in some past life by their perception, done some terrible deed with their hands. They also could have been a very grasping person, wanting everything for themselves.

Now, this will manifest in any form of inability to use your hands, whether it be through **arthritis** or...what is that other...tunnel syndrome? **Carpal tunnel syndrome**. What they call ballpark elbow...no, that's not quite right. **Tennis elbow**, all right. I knew it had something to do with balls and games, anyway.

So, anything that works against movement or grasping stems from a fear that they cannot grasp or that they have been overly grasping and need to be stopped from grasping, and so they will develop various and sundry ailments that will keep ...

The **elbow** also represents your flexibility. How flexible are you? If your elbow is stiff or painful, it means that you are unwilling to *yield* in some area. You are not willing to perhaps give the benefit of the doubt or perhaps allow another to have their own way or perhaps just you're going to do it your way no matter what. What is that...you have a melody upon your earth, "I Did It My Way"? (Laughter) People who think like that frequently develop elbow and wrist problems.

The **pelvic area** is very different in men and women. Men's pelvis is narrower and more solid because a man has a heavier body to support. A man must do, by the concepts of people, must do laborious work.

So the pelvic area in men and women is very different. A man with pelvic problems usually questions his manhood, and I don't mean it sexually necessarily, but perhaps questions his ability to be like a man, to act like a man, to support his family perhaps, or to take charge of things. And this can represent any manner of problems through the pelvic area. **Prostate cancer** is one. **Inability to perform sexually** is another. **Inability to relieve himself** of body fluids is another. Anything that would be a problem in that area usually stems from the fear that he is not man enough for the task at hand, regardless of what it might be.

A woman who has problems in that area, if it is **uterine** or has to do with **childbearing**, that stems from a fear of having children or fear of not being a good mother, a fear of having to carry someone else. A fear of—and it doesn't have to mean a pregnancy necessarily—but a fear of being responsible for someone that you don't want to have to carry along and nurture. It also stems from a feeling that *you* are not nurtured. A woman who feels unloved or undesirable frequently will develop **cancer of the uterus** or of the **reproductive organs**.

A person who has bowel, **lower bowel problems**, finds it very difficult to release and let go of old hurts. They tend to be unforgiving, not in a malicious way, but simply in a "I'm not ever going to do that again," or "I'm not ever going to love that person again because if I do, they will hurt me." Feelings of betrayal most often represent themselves in the lower bowel because that is one of the things you need to realize is an illusion and doesn't ever really happen. You've agreed to it or it wouldn't have come to you, and you need to release it and let it go.

The **upper legs**...**thighs**? And what is the name of the bone? The femur? **Femur**. Ah, you got that one wrong, yes you did! (Laughter) I know you said thighbone but there is another name there, you see? It doesn't matter. Let me go on with my lesson now.

Now, this attaches to the body. This is a very important bone because it has to be strong because that's what's going to make you able to move forward. This is what attaches to your hip socket. Get a little hip socket in here. [Draws]

Now, the **hip socket** is one of the places where most people develop problems as they get older, and why? Because as people get older, they get set in their ways and a person who is set in their ways doesn't like to change direction. They don't like to move away from where they are headed and when it is required of them to do so, they frequently refuse. So what is happening is the urge to turn and go another way is coming and they're steadfastly, "No, I'm going *that* way." So, here instead of moving and being flexible, there comes a rigidity. "I'm *not* going. I *won't* move." And it manifests in one of the most important places in the body. You can't move forward if your hips aren't working right, can you? Oh, you could hop like a bunny rabbit I suppose, but you need flexibility in your hips to walk and certainly walking represents moving forward. So, when it's time for you to move on and you don't want to move on, you can expect to have problems in your hips. Now, sometimes it's merely a problem that comes from the spine, needs a new alignment, all the way to where you have to have hips rebuilt or redone over.

Now the **thighbone**, femur bone...that is your connectedness to flexibility. That's the bone that's going to be supportive of your movement, that's going to allow you to take that step, to move that hip bone.

And when there's problems in here, usually that represents a great deal of terror of the future. What is in the future? What if something is lurking there waiting to get me? What if, what if, what if? And so the person, rather than move forward and take a chance of something terrible awaiting them, they would develop ailments or perhaps break these bones so that they can't move forward *unless someone else takes them.* So, a fear of moving forward on one's own usually manifests in bone problems of the femur.

Knees. [Draws] I don't know. I never looked. She [Tinkerbell] asked me if I ever looked at a bee's knees and seen how cute they were. (Laughter) Has anyone ever looked at a bee's knees? Don't think so, no.

Knees also represent flexibility but knees also represent your ability to come down and to stand up. People with **knee problems**...again that's a different kind of inflexibility. You know how some people are going to do what they are going to do no matter what happens? They are so stubborn that you cannot get through to them about anything. "No, it's this way." That's in the hip area.

People with problems with the knees *will change* albeit not without a fight and not without a lot of, "All right, I'll do it your way but I don't *want* to." And they sort of move forward with a shuffling. They're not willing.

It also represents your ability to bow before a higher power. In just about every religion upon the earth, prayer is done in either a kneeling position or a prone position or somehow bowed down. Bending of the knee represents your agreement that there is a divine being.

Now, it may be that you believe there is a divine being but it may be that you believe that divine being is judgmental and out to get you. How many of you going to parochial school or to Sunday school when you were growing up were told, "If you chewed gum, God's going to get you. If you tell a lie, God's going to get you. If you do this or that, God's going to get you"? So you are taught that God's just sitting there waiting, *hoping* for you to do some *terrible* thing so He can say, "Ah ha! Zap!" (Laughter)

Unwillingness to bow before a god like that, which...I wouldn't bow before a god like that either. But since as children you are taught that that's the only God there is, you grow up, you resent that. You resent having a god that *waits* for you to do something terrible. You resent having a god that's going to get you for every little infraction of justice. Let me ask you, what god in his right mind would punish a child for chewing gum in church? I don't know any, but are you not taught that?

So, the knees represent how you think God is, in a sense, or your concept of whether you are in favor or out of favor with God, your willingness or unwillingness to yield on bended knee.

It also represents your dominant nature. If you are a dominant person, you're not going to bend knee to anyone or anything. So therefore, any forced...anytime someone comes in and is dominant over you through force, such as one country being overtaken with another country, there's knee problems.

Religious people who enter into contracts with the church—nuns and monks and so forth who spend a lot of time kneeling—after many years, a lot of them get resentful of the authority of the church over them and they develop knee problems to the point where they have to leave the convent or the monastery because they can't kneel any longer. Now, that to them constitutes God throwing them out.

The **leg bone**. Now this leg bone comes in two pieces. You have the main leg bone and then you have a little bone off to the side, and what are they called?

Participant: I knew you were going to ask me. The **tibia** and the **fibula**.

Gabriel: And which is which?

Participant: Uh, I can't remember. The tibia is the one on top.

Gabriel: The tibia is the main bone? The tibia is the little bowey bone and the fibia is the larger bone?

Participant: The tibia is the big one and the fibula is...

Gabriel: So it's the other way around from what I just said?

Participant: Yes.

Gabriel: Don't pay any attention to me! I don't know one bone from the other.

Now, the main bone of your leg, whatever it be called—Oscar, shall we? Perhaps call it Oscar?—now that bone, if you break it, you can't step upon your leg but if you break the little side bone, if you have a cast on it, you can step upon your leg.

So, breaking of the main bone—or injury thereof or disease thereof—would represent a fear of having to hold one's own weight or carry your own weight or be responsible for your responsibilities. This little side bone represents the annoyances in your life that you depend upon to keep you miserable. (Laughter) Oh, everyone has them, you know.

You do have interruptions in your life that you subconsciously depend upon to be your reason why you can't do this or you're late for that or you had better not attempt to do this because you know you are not going to have the time. Anybody here in that category? (Laughter)

Now, the thing is, this little bone, while it is important, you can go on with your life if something happens to it. You can go on because you have your main... So, what you have here is your main concept and then you have the annoyances that you have invited into your life to allow you time to not do what you don't want to do.

And all of you volunteer for things you *really* don't want to do, don't you? Because you've all got guilty consciences. You all fall under the whip of, "Well, if I don't, what will they think," or "I had better because so-and-so can't, so therefore it falls to me. I don't want to do it. Oh well, I'll do it all right." That little bone represents all of that attitude.

Now we come to the **ankles**. Ankles are an interesting thing. You can move your foot in every which way because of your ankle. They also represent deception in your life, not necessarily *your* deception. It could be a feeling of having been deceived by someone or it also could be your feeling that you have deceived someone, perhaps without intent, but nonetheless you tell them something, it turns out not to be true and you feel, "Oh gee, I went and told them this or that. Now look. Now I've deceived them. I don't want to deceive them."

One of Beloved Woman's things we had to work with her on when all this channeling business started...it left her very fearful, very fearful. And I said to her one day, "Beloved Woman, what are you afraid of? Are you afraid of appearing to be a fool?" She said, "No, I don't ever want to lead anyone astray. I don't ever want to deceive them." And I said, "Why do you think you would be deceiving them?" She said, "Because what if, in the end, you aren't Gabriel after all? And what if you had been teaching them things that aren't so?"

I said, "And what if that proved true? What if? What if? Let's go with your what if." Then, she said, "I would be the great deceiver. I would have deceived people all my life long and I don't ever want to lead anyone astray. I would rather have them never believe me than to have one false thing come through my mouth, whether it be of my own doing or of your doing." She said, "I don't ever want to consciously or unconsciously lead anyone astray."

When you feel that is happening, whether it be justified or not, whether you be the deceiver or someone deceives you, you will sustain an ankle injury. Know you how you have a phrase, you turned your ankle, you strained your ankle, sprained your ankle, or broke your ankle or something. Usually you can trace that kind of an injury or ailment to a feeling of either having been deceived or have inadvertently deceived.

Now I assured her she would...and she was always turning her ankle. "What did you do?" "I turned my ankle." "Ah," says I, "and who do you think is deceiving whom?" "Well, I don't know." Well, as the years passed she come to realize that no one was being deceived, including herself, so the ankle injuries stopped.

Feet and **eyes** both represent understanding.

Know you how you use the term when someone is explaining something to you and you understand and you say, "Oh, I see what you're saying"? You aren't actually *seeing* what they're saying. What you mean is you understand it.

The feet also represent understanding because you walk upon them. Your understanding is what carries you forward in life. You go in the direction your understanding takes you. So feet and eyes, up here... How you perceive the world and the conclusions you come to thereof are represented by the eyes. Your understanding is what you go forward with into the world, so both of these have very similar meaning.

A person who is sighted by the far...no, that's not how you say it...**farsighted** usually believes in the goodness of the future but doesn't want to look at what's under their nose right now. A person who is close...**nearsighted** is someone who fears the future and feels that the only thing they can depend upon is this very present moment so what's closest to them is dependable. What's in the future, heaven only knows.

People who have other ailments...

[Someone opens a door to the outside.] I see the spirit of the wind is out in full force today having a ball, I guess. Tinkerbell says, "No, a whole flock of angels just went by at top speed." (Laughter) Whatever.

People with **eye problems**, whether it be...I don't know your terms. Name me some eye ailments. **Cataracts**, **glaucoma**, anything that prohibits you from seeing, usually it's because you feel you don't want to look. It's got to be so bad out there that you don't want to look. Now, that's all subconscious. It's not a conscious thing.

People who have difficulty with the **ears**, who can't hear, usually have had a childhood in which they didn't want to hear what was going on around them. Children who go to bed at night and then listen to Mommy and Daddy scream and yell at each other or Daddy beat up Mommy or whatever usually don't want to hear that, and it will produce difficulty in hearing.

People who also don't want to take in new ideas, who don't want to hear what the world has to offer, they also will have difficulty in hearing. Anything that blocks out sound that would be disturbing to them, they have problems hearing.

Oh, she does? Tinkerbell reminds me Beloved Woman wears two hearing appendages. That goes to her older childhood where she didn't want to hear what was going on in the household.

The **toes** represent the details of your life. Now, not too many people give serious thought to details in their life. I could go to anyone of you and say, "Name me a detail in your life," and you'd sit there, "Uh, uh, I don't know." You can't think of a detail in your life.

Let me tell you what details of your life are. Do you feel it's absolutely imperative that you make your bed straight away after you rise in the morn? (Laughter) What if your floor isn't swept or your car isn't bathed or your dog has fleas or your cat hairballs? All right, we get the drift. (Laughter) Those are the details of your life, the little things.

You start out in the morning and then you remember...you can't remember if you shut your apparatus that smooths your clothes off. Or did you turn off the shower? Or did you turn off the stove with the teakettle upon it? Those are the little details of life that get your attention and hold onto it.

We have watched the ladies belabor themselves over what color coating they should put upon the ends of their fingers. (Laughter) "What am I going to be wearing for the next week because I've got to pick a color that goes with everything that I'd be wearing? Well, I'd better figure that out first. Then I'll put this color on. No, I'd better not." And they spend perhaps a half hour or an hour or more just selecting the color of the paint on their fingers. Same way with whatever they put upon their mouth there.

The gentlemen, those who care, (laughter) belabor over what tie might go with what shirt and what shirt goes with what trousers and what shoes go with what socks and all that sort of thing. Those are the details of your life. They aren't bad. They're not wrong. They're just the little details of your life.

People who have toe problems—whether it be **arthritis** or whatever, **calluses** or **corns** or something, **bunions** and all that sort of thing— represent over-concern about the details of life. You are much too much embroiled in the little unnecessary necessities, and so that will bring about that problem.

Now, all of this that I have said goes back to one thing: **fear**. You can take anything that I have talked about and its basis will be fear. People are afraid of the strangest things. The obvious things are afraid of the dark, afraid of spiders, afraid of this or that, but it is the subconscious fear that really governs your lives. And every one of you, every person upon the earth, has one major fear and that is that they are not loveable. They don't deserve to be loved and they certainly aren't ever going to truly be loved, even if there are very loving people in their world, even if they have a loving mate or had loving parents or loving children, loving friends. If they don't feel that they are lovable, they will do things—subconsciously they will do things—to make that love go away or to feel that they are not worthy of it.

How many of you in this room feel that you are absolutely, totally, one hundred percent lovable all the time? (Laughter) I didn't see any hands go up at all. But do you know what I am saying about that? You have times when you feel very lovable. Then you have times when you don't feel you're lovable at all. And most of the time, you feel unlovable.

How many of you feel that someone else in your family is far more lovable than you are? (Laughter) When someone says, "I love you," the average person thinks, "I'm so lucky because if they really knew me..." "Why wouldn't they love you?" "Well, because." "Because why?" "Well, just because." "Name me something." "Well, I'm too tall or I'm too short or I'm too fat or I'm too thin or I'm not smart enough or I never went to college or I don't know how to play baseball or..." What is that other term? "I'm not good in bed." I could never figure that one out! (Laughter) The only thing about going to bed is you go in, you lie down, you put your head on your pillow, and you go to sleep. Oh, that's not all? (Laughter) All right. Whatever.

The thing is that you all have some reason why you think that you aren't lovable and that is the basis behind all of these things that I have talked of this day with you...is the fear that you are not lovable. "What if they won't keep me?" Whoever *they* may be. "What if they won't keep me?"

When Beloved Woman was a little girl, they lived upon a farm—had many animals, cows and so forth—and she worked very, very hard, not because she was told to, but because she felt she had to because if she didn't, *they* wouldn't keep her. She cleaned after, I forgot how many, almost sixty or seventy head of cattle with a shovel by herself and she is the only one who did it. Her father never told her she had to do that but she did it. She kept the barn spotlessly clean because she feared if she didn't, that somehow they would not keep her. Now, neither of her parents knew anything about this. She wasn't even conscious of it but that was her fear.

And everyone has a similar type of fear, maybe not be manifested in that way, but it goes all the way back to the idea that you all think you left God and He's *really* upset with you. He's really angry because you walked out of paradise with not so much as a thank you very much. That never happened but you have been taught that's what happened. So, you have this fear.

Now you are learning that you are lovable. You are learning that God doesn't hold *anything* against you, that you have the right to use your power, that you have the right and the ability to heal, but you're still grappling with that because you're not lovable.

Now, if you are going to heal people, then you have to know why they're sick, why they're hurt, where the wounds are. You have to recognize—only inasmuch as it gives you a sense of direction with your healing—but you have to recognize the areas of the body and what they represent because the physical body is *only* the out-picturing of the higher concept of yourself.

So, wherever your problem is or their problem is, you can know that that's the area that needs healing, not in the physical body, but you have to get to the cause. And once you heal the cause, the physical body will be healed. It has to be. Just as when you get your vertebrae properly aligned so that the energy can come through unto the nerves and nourish the organs that they're meant to, that heals the organs. Getting rid of the breakage of the cause of the problem in their belief system will automatically heal the body.

You don't have to say to them, "Oh, you have a problem in your back here or there and so that's going to be...you are afraid of thus-and-so." Some people you can say that to; other people you cannot. But direct your healing not to the outer manifestation—that will get temporary results—direct your healing to the cause. You don't have to tell them that's what you're doing if they are the type of person who wouldn't accept it, but directing your healing to the cause of the problem is going to give them permanent healing because it's going to remove why the problem is happening. And that's what healing is about. It's getting at the cause. Teaching them that they are loved by God just as they are this very moment is another form of healing.

Now, have you anything to ask of me?

Participant: There are those of us who have followed you in the years and done the lessons that you have taught and we believe what you say and we take it to heart. But still there seems to be something that hasn't clicked because we still find ourselves in a mess.

Gabriel: Well, being in the mess usually has two causes. One, some aspect of you enjoys the adventure, or you don't feel worthy of getting out of the mess. You don't feel that you are deserving of being released from its grasp upon you.

Now, most people it is because they enjoy, on another level, the adventure. "How smart am I? Can I get out of this mess? I can get out of this mess." But the conscious personality part of you is struggling with the mess and saying, "Oh, what shall I do?" while the other part of you is saying, "You're smart enough. You can get out of it." Now, which are you? (Laughter)

Participant: Well, I'm still in the mess so I don't know. (Laughter) I had found on one of your tapes though, the saying, "From the heart of me, I accept the love of God." And the repetition of that, God being everything, eventually I will accept the love of God and therefore everything.

Gabriel: As soon as you accept the will of God, you're going to find the mess is gone, has disappeared, because it has no further purpose. Its only purpose is to keep you convinced that God doesn't love you or you wouldn't be in the mess you're in.

I would tell you, beloved entity, but if I did I would open Pandora's Box. Then every single person would get up and want me to tell them what their problem was. So because of that, I shan't tell you, but suffice it to say it this way... You can't save the world; you can only save yourself. And you know what I'm talking about, do you not?

Participant: Well, I'll dwell on that.

Gabriel: You dwell on it...*rescuer*. (Laughter)

Participant: Could you give me the nature of the ego and the proper use of it in our lives?

Gabriel: The nature of ego and ...?

Participant: ...the proper use and balance in our lives of ego.

Gabriel: The balance in your life with your ego is your God Self, is your ability to take in and utilize the "I Am a child of God-ness" in you. The ego will always approach you with fear, even if it is little fears like doubts or not sure of yourself. The ego will never come up and say, "Boo!" at you because it doesn't want to frighten you openly because then you've got defenses, so it sneaks around and presents itself in little ways.

When you know the ego is after you, say to the ego, "I am the Son of God and *you* are my servant so get thee behind me. I have no need of you now," even if you have to do it a hundred times a day. The ego will sneak up on you.

If nothing else, you can be driving your mode of transportation and someone will cut in front of you and you get angry and you think, "You miserable so-and-so." That's the ego chalking one up, "Got him that time." Now, when that happens, you think, "No, I'm not going to buy into this. So the person cut in front of me. So what? I'm all right. They're all right. No big deal." That defeats the ego.

Not allowing yourself to get upset over delays or... The ego is so subtle. It never comes out openly. It always sneaks around in little ways that you *think* it's not the ego.

For example, let us say you have to be a certain place a certain time and you are about to go out the door so that you will not be late, and the phone rings and you answer and a friend says, "Oh, I'm in terrible mess. Can you just talk with me for five minutes? I just need you to assure me da da, da da...," and you think, "Well, I really ought to go but..." The ego says, "But you're a healer! You have to listen to this person. You can't say, 'I'm sorry. I can't talk to you now. Let me call you later. I'll be very happy to hear you later. Right now, I have to do thus-and-so.'"

No. The ego uses your guilty conscience and you're standing there on the phone *really* not *wanting* to help the person when looking at your clock and thinking, "I'm going to be late." Then you dash out the door and you're angry with the drivers on the road and you're angry with yourself and you're very angry with that person...

Now, where has the healing been? None. There is none. But if you were to say to that person, "I really can't talk to you at this moment. I do love you very much and I want very much to help you. Let me go and tend to my business and when I get back, I'll call you straight away." Then when you come home, you're relaxed and you can talk and then there's healing. But when you're doing it on the fly and you're very upset, you're not helping anybody and that's the work of the ego.

Participant: When we have an illness—disease, broken bone, whatever—is it helpful to say, "What fear am I responding to?"

Gabriel: When you have an illness or a broken bone, is it helpful to say, "What fear am I responding to?" Yes, it 'tis.

Participant: And then we can go consciously through what we think that fear might be and this would be helpful?

Gabriel: You can go consciously through that fear and everything would be helpful, yes.

Participant: If we cannot find the answer, a conscious answer, can we ask the Holy Spirit to remove that fear from us without us being conscious of it?

Gabriel: If you cannot consciously touch into the fear, can you ask the Holy Spirit to take it away? Absolutely. All you have to do is say, "This gathering of energy that has manifested as a fear, I ask you, Holy Spirit, to transform it into a blessing. I release it and I give it unto you." And the Holy Spirit gladly takes it up to the higher realms and transforms it.

Participant: Gabriel, many times when people come to me seeking counsel, they come with their pain and their fear about not being loved. And many times it takes the form of them wanting to have the perfect boyfriend or girlfriend or husband or wife and they're looking for love and yet it seems that they will have an active social life and they may even have an active social, physical, sexual life, but it's like nobody ever measures up or they're always being rejected by this other person. And I know it has to do with allowing love and allowing intimacy. How would you suggest we, or I, in working with people because it's such a perennial issue, what way, verbally, might we assist them in their healing if they want it, and what would be the cause of that?

Gabriel: The cause is always the same: the fear that God doesn't love them, the fear they are unlovable. So they're going to sabotage any relationship, be it of man/woman or friendship or brother and sister or parent or sibling or child, whatever, because they feel that's all they deserve is the secondhand, almost-as-good-but-not-quite kind of love. So no matter who came along and loved them, they're going to find a way of sabotaging it.

So what they need to recognize is their method of sabotage. Now, some people will use the method of, "Well, I know he loves me but I wish he were someone else. I wish he was the fellow that used to love me. Why can't it be that guy who loves me instead of this guy who loves me?" Now, that is one way of putting love off. What they need to know, the person who is loving them now is the best person for where they are at this moment and to release the past and accept the love that is there.

"Oh, but he's not tall enough." Tall enough for what? Do you want him to wash the windows of the second story of your building or what? (Laughter) They will find that he or she is not this or that enough. "You don't need that in your life right now because if you did, it would be there." Help them to see that what is presented to them in love is where they...that's what they need at the moment. That's where they are at. Now, it's up to them to do it. You can't do it for them.

Participant: No, I know that. Thank you.

Participant: Gabriel, many of our students here will be going on to be ordained ministers to help in some way and whether they are or not, a lot of them may be put in situations in the future where they may be supportive of or assisting people to pass from their physical bodies to the spirit world. And when a lot of people...some of my experiences I've come across where people have been very fearful of not being worthy to go to God. And I wondered if you could address that for some of the people here, please. Could you give us some helpful suggestions?

Gabriel: The question was how does one deal with a situation where they are administering to a dying person and the person is afraid to die because they fear they will not get to see God.

You might point out to them that God gave them life in the beginning and the only purpose that God gave them life was because God loved them into being-ness. And because they were loved into being-ness, they have always been loved. And because they have always been loved, the only thing that's different is that they are being loved without a body. And the only thing that's changing is that they will no longer be encased in a physical form. But the love that has ever been with them is with them eternally.

Participant: Thank you.

Gabriel: I'm going to tell a little story on Beloved Woman. I'm not sure she would want me to but she'll get over it. (Laughter) One day in her home, she was busy about her household chores. I guess she was doing laundry and she bumped into an invisible form in the doorway and she stopped and she backed up and she was looking like this and didn't see anything, but there was something blocking her passage in the doorway. So she set down her basket and she is going like this [puts hands out] and she felt herself touch someone's chest and she could feel shoulders and so forth, so she stepped back and she said, "If you are not of God, in the name of Christ, leave," and she heard a hearty laugh and she looked and there stood the Master Jesus.

And she was so taken aback by it, she said, "Oh," she said, "I didn't see you." And he said, "That's because you weren't looking for me," which she wasn't. She was doing her laundry. So he reached out and, as he is wont to do with people, he put his arms around her and he held her to him. She said, "You're holding me." She was so amazed at this. She said, "You're holding me," and he said, "I've always held you."

And that is a grand truth. Whether you believe in the Master Jesus or in Buddha, it doesn't make any difference, the love of God will find a way of *holding* you and of making you know you are being held. You have to expect it.

Now, when she does her laundry, she picks up her laundry basket, she puts in on her hip, and she's going like this [puts hands out] through the doorway. (Laughter) He hasn't come back to repeat it, much to her disappointment, but the point I'm getting at is that love is never absent from you, ever—never, ever absent from you. Even in your most distressed state, that love ever embraces you, ever sustains you, ever *holds* you. So when he said, "I have always held you," he was speaking for God. God *always holds you,* whether you are in the flesh or whether you are in the spirit world. It doesn't make any difference. And that is something you must remember always. You are ever, ever being held.

Any other questions?

Participant: Will you speak to the root cause of chronic sinus problems?

Gabriel: The root cause of **chronic sinus problems**, yes. Congested thinking.

Your sinuses are air passages in the skull, which add to your balance. It gives you...it adds to your ability to know what direction you're walking in and to not fall over. When your thoughts are going in a thousand directions at once or when you're trying to, in your perception, to solve a lot of problems all at the same time or there's a lot of demands upon you...people are asking, "Would you want this? Should we do that? Da da, da da," and you are trying to...you're scattering your energies. That causes congestion in the sinuses because number one, you feel overwhelmed. Number two, you don't have a good sense of your own direction and you're out of balance with yourself, so that will produce all in here and up in here and even down by your ears.

Participant: Would you speak to allergies, please?

Gabriel: Allergies, the root cause of **allergies**. "Why am I here? Why am I not somewhere else? Why am I so out of tune with my environment? Why am I not at peace in my world?"

Participant: Gabriel, as was mentioned, this class is going to be graduating and whether they choose ordination formally or not, if there was one thing that you would have to say to them or share with them as they go out to minister, what might you share with them to carry forth in their work and in their life?

Gabriel: Always teach truth, always heal from your highest self, and *always* love what you do. If you follow those three things, you will be successful in what you do.

Participant: Thank you once again so much.

Participant: Can you talk to us about guardian angels? What roles they play?

Gabriel: Guardian angels are just what they say. They're guardians. They don't interfere with your free will. They will guide you and guard you in whatever path you choose to walk. They influence you. They do not command you. They will suggest or influence but they don't ever make you do or not do something. And they always love you to pieces. Always.

Participant: [Inaudible]

Gabriel: The **skin** is an organ that...well, one thing it holds you all together. Otherwise your parts would be all over the place. (Laughter) The other thing it does, it is one of your sensory organs and perhaps it is one of the most sensitive because you can feel even a slight breeze upon your skin. So it represents your sensitivity to your world. It represents your ability to be sensitive to and to be aware of what's going on about you.

Participant: Could you address children who take on the illness of their parents and what's the best way to help them so they don't need to do that?

Gabriel: Children who take on almost any kind of ailment, whether it be the ailments of their parents...children take on ailments of parents usually are parroting the parents because they feel that's what they're supposed to do. "Mommy or Daddy did it so that's what I'm supposed to do." But children who are ill usually feel very insecure and they feel the only way they can keep the attention of their parents and the safety of the care of their parents is to be incapacitated, to have to be taken care of.

Participant: I understand that as healers, from what we learned this morning, it benefits us to not focus on the specific ailment but rather focus on the individual that we're helping having perfect health.

Gabriel: True.

Participant: So, is where this cause stuff comes in, is that...like obviously, we're supposed to focus on the cause. Do we do this verbally or where does that come into the ...

Gabriel: It depends upon the person. Some people you can say, "This represents thus-and-so. Therefore, your cause is in this area," and they will understand. Other people, they don't want to know nothing from nothing. They just want you to make them better. So it depends.

Now, you still see the person perfect. You don't deviate from that, but knowing where they're coming from in producing this illness...and you can talk to them about it. You can say to them, "I feel you have a great fear in this area and you really need to think about that. Think healing thoughts to yourself concerning this," and then see them perfect.

Participant: Lung cancer. What fear would cause that, but also what about **smoking** and **eating different foods**?

Gabriel: It's all a cause. When a person deliberately does things to harm their body such as smoking or whatever, it is their way of saying to God, "To heck with You. This is my body. I'm going to do whatever I please with it and if You don't like it, I don't care." Now, what they are really doing is saying that to life. "I don't care." They are refusing to take in life and they are going to *guarantee* that they can't take in life by destroying their lungs.

Participant: The world is [inaudible] for the rest of this year.

Gabriel: That's a lengthy one. (Laughter)

Participant: I did save it for last!

Gabriel: I'll just go briefly. This is the year of rapid transition. This is the year when everything will change very rapidly. A lot of earth changes will happen this year, have already begun, already started. A lot of long-standing systems in your world will collapse and new systems will have to come about.

My Father, for these,
Thy blessed, blessed children,
I give You thanks.

This time upon the earth with them
has brought great joy to my heart.
I know, Father God,
they are keenly aware of Your love, oh Your love,

154

Healing in the World

Your love that wraps around,
embraces, sustains, and gives life.
May they never feel that You are not with them.

Bless them, Father God,
with the integrity of the teachings
they have been given,
that as they go forth to lay on hands,
to speak the word, to heal,
that they may see how their efforts are bringing
about a change in consciousness.
How it is not only the bodies that are healed
but the minds and the souls as well.
And ever, Father God,
grant them Your peace.

And so it is.

And I shall see you again.

How Healing Happens
November 6, 1998

Archangel Gabriel: Tonight we are going to talk about the various ways in which healing happens to the person. [Gabriel draws.] We'll put some clothes on this creature. Pointy ears...it's Mister Spock. (Laughter)

All healing comes from God who works through your doctors. The healing process takes place first in your soul, then in your mind, and then in your body. Your emotions enter in there in various and sundry ways and we shall discuss this night how all of these things work to make you a healthy person.

The mind and the soul have the most powerful effect upon your healing, much more powerful than anything else, because your attitude toward yourself determines whether or not you are going to allow your body or your mind or your emotions, whatever part of you might be ill, to take in and utilize the perfect health that is all around you from God.

You dwell in a sea of vibrational rates and you dwell in your aura, which is of God. You are in this egg, which is your aura and the whole capsule is contained within the power and the presence of God. So healing is all around about you. It doesn't matter where you are. Healing is surrounding you. Perfect health is surrounding you at all times.

Now, we're going to start with the part of you that you are most familiar with. We're going to start with the part where you go to the doctor and he prescribes some very, very expensive medication.

Now that heals two things...your body and his wallet. (Laughter) Now, are there any doctors present? If so, I apologize.

Now, when you take medication into your body, it has to work first in the body, of course. The stomach digests it or the bloodstream carries it, however it is administered to you, and it will travel to the place where the healing is needed. I'm not going to get into different healings or different illnesses. Rather, I'm just going to talk about healing.

Now, because it approaches the avenue of wellness from the physical, it's kind of like swimming upstream, in a way, because it first affects the body. Now this isn't bad because when your body is at rest—in other words, when your body is not in pain or not in discomfort—it allows the mind and soul to function more freely. It frees up your thought process and this is so important because the body will do what the mind tells it to, regardless. It will do what the mind tells it to and it doesn't matter what kind of medication you are taking, if your thought process is that you are not going to be well, then you can take all the medication in the world and you will not be well because the body will only take and utilize it for a certain length of time and then it will reject the effects of it because the mind of you is telling it to do that.

Let us assume that you have taken a quantity of medication into your body. The mind of you sends in a thought process into your brain... You have taken in your medication. Now, the mind will send in thoughts for you to consider and those thoughts would be, "Well, I'm feeling better. I think I shall be all right. I will be fine. I know I shall be fine." Now, that comes into your thought process.

Now you have emotions who come in here. Now, let us suppose you've got a very positive thought. Let us suppose the mind has said to you, "Well, your body's feeling better. This medication is going to work. You're going to be just fine."

Now in come the emotions. "Well, Great Aunt Suzanne had this very ailment and she perished. Maybe I shall too. Maybe feeling good is only temporary. I wonder if I ought to call my doctor and find out if there are any side effects to this medication that could be damaging to me elsewhere in my body." So now you've got worry thoughts filled with emotion. That emotion is fear.

Now, these two things combined—the power of the mind and the power of emotions—they're going to tell the body, "Maybe you're not as well as you think you are. Maybe you're going to have some side effects. Maybe this isn't a good idea. You know, Great Aunt Suzanne...she was gone. You'd best be very careful." Now the body is getting a second signal here, "You're not all right." So the body has to bypass, and it will, the effects of the medication and it will revert back to the reason why you went to the doctor in the first place.

And this is why a lot of people get well to a certain degree and then they get worse and then they get a little better and then they get worse. And they go back and forth and back and forth because they have the mind and the emotions working together to attack any idea that the body had that the medication that was given to it was good. Now, that's one way that that works.

Let us suppose that you are in a situation that you are very unhappy with—maybe your job, marriage, combination thereof, or lack thereof of both, whatever—but whatever it is, you're subconsciously not in a good place, and while you consciously think, "Oh, I shall be fine," in your soul is the memory of *everything* you have ever said, thought, felt, or done— everything, everything, everything—right from the get-go. Your soul is a permanent, perfect memory.

Now, in the soul is a past experience with an illness similar—or perhaps exactly the same, who knows—that you went through in another lifetime, maybe four or five lifetimes ago, and you were sick unto death. You died.

Now, you also have in your soul's memory the reason why you came to the earth in this particular incarnation. You have in that soul's memory all of what you have come here to learn, to teach, to accomplish, to grow.

And that soul memory knows that at any point you can change your mind, and you can choose whether to stay here on the earth or to leave. Now, that is very rarely ever, ever a conscious decision. Very few people ever consciously say, "I think I'll die," and actually do it. That kind of direction comes from the soul. It does not come from the conscious mind and it does not come from the emotions. That kind of decision is a *soul* decision and it is made within your soul by your *higher mind*.

Now, let us suppose that you are in this situation that's not earth shattering but you are not happy. You haven't been happy for a long time and you get an illness. Now, here presents an opportunity for you to leave the earth or to greatly, vastly change your way of life—doesn't always have to be in death—and the soul feeds into your subconscious mind, which is in the solar plexus, an option; you don't have to get well if you don't want to. You can get partially well or you can pass over into spirit, whichever you decide, and it's your decision.

Now, there has to be created for you a time element. Let's put the time element up here. [Draws] Now, there has to be created in your subconscious—in your mind, in your soul, in all of these things here—there has to be created a space for you to think and feel this through.

Now, people find a way of taking that space when they are making a decision. Some people will go into, what you term in your day and time, a **coma** and they will linger there sometimes for several days, a week, or more while they decide what to do with the options that they have. Some people will just simply sleep a lot...long, long hours of sleep.

While they are sleeping, they have journeyed out of the body and up into their higher self. They have communed with their soul and they can see what lies in the future for them with this option, with that option, and with another option. They can also determine whether the body is going to sufficiently recuperate to serve them if they should decide to remain upon the earth, because sometimes the body is damaged beyond repair and couldn't serve them well at all, in which case they almost always decide to leave the earth.

However, they also may decide that the situation they are in would be too painful for them to change, to alter, so that cuts down their options. Now they can decide to either leave the earth or to remain on the earth and to continue on in the process that they have become familiar with, even though they hate it, and you'd be surprised the number of people who choose to do exactly that.

When they choose to do that, they usually leave themselves an open door and somewhere down the road—three, four, five, ten years later—they will present to their body another opportunity to leave the earth, and when they choose to do that, they usually do leave.

Now all of this—your body—is the direct receiver of all of these instructions from the soul, from the mind, the emotions. Your body does not think for itself as far as making decisions is concerned. It has a sense of survival and given half a chance will certainly live on. But if the instrument of its information is telling it, "I'm not sure I want to stay. This is a very iffy situation.

I just may choose to leave later on," the body will remain...will maintain within the cell structure of it...

Now remember, your cells are living things. They are living things. They are spirit in form. It will retain within the physical form a cellular seed that it will keep in abeyance until such time as the person decides they want to leave. Then, that seed in the cells becomes activated. It's given direction by the mind, emotions, by the soul, and it will reactivate itself and it will produce an illness that will bring death.

Now, these are decisions that every single individual upon your earth makes many, many times in one lifetime. It is not something that happens to a few. It is not something that happens only to people who have terminal...what you call terminal illnesses. It is something that everyone decides many times over in your life. You would be surprised the number of times little children make that very decision of whether to stay or to go.

Now, let us bypass medicine. Let us suppose that you are awakened enough, illumined enough, to know that there is divine healing. Let us suppose that you go to a healing practitioner or healer, whatever you want to call it, or you belong to a healing group or you call a prayer group or something and you say, "I am very ill. I have thus-and-so and I need your prayers." All right, you get four or five thousand people praying for you. Now what do you think that's going to do?

"Where there are two or more gathered in My name, there am I in the midst of them." If you think that the prayer power of even four or five people is not much, you are very sadly mistaken. Where *two* people are gathered with *one thought*, the thought of healing someone, the power of those two people, if it could be transformed into electricity, would light up your city.

Now, if you add to that the prayers of several hundred people or several thousand people, there is no way that that healing power isn't going to heal that body, *except* if in the soul, the mind, there is no acceptance of it.

Now, I want to show you about healing power. The moment one person, *one person,* says a prayer of healing for another, that healing power is drawn like a magnet and it approaches the aura of the person being prayed for but it does not enter. It does not enter. Now, the only way that healing power can enter and do its work is by *invitation of the person being prayed for.*

You could have Jesus, the Master, come down and lay his hands upon you to heal you and if in your soul and mind you said, "I don't want it," you wouldn't get it. *You* are the deciding factor as to whether the healing works or doesn't work. There is no such thing as a bad healer. There is no such thing as unanswered prayer. There is no such thing as someone not getting the healing that is being sent to them, up to the point of the periphery of their aura.

Now, once healing has been sent, that healing never leaves that person, *ever*. It will follow them several lifetimes into the future. It will stay with them until such time as that person chooses to open themselves and let it in, and then it comes in two places. It comes into the solar plexus and it comes in in the back of your head. Back here is the place of entrance for anything of a spiritual nature, and in the solar plexus.

When the person decides to accept the healing... Now, here's the other thing. They can choose to accept *all* of the healing and be healed instantly or they can choose to accept enough healing to get to feel better but not one hundred percent because they want a little reserve. They want to keep a little bit under the weather just in case they change their mind and want to leave. And some people take many years to think it over, many years to make that decision.

Now, when healing surrounds the aura, it waits for any opportunity, even if there's just an itsy-bitsy hole in the aura, even if one day the person thinks, "You know...maybe I will stay. Maybe if I felt better, I'd want to stay. Maybe I'll be healed. Maybe I'll let this work," a little bit of hole, a little place opens up, and the healing rushes in.

Okay, now why would healing wait? Why wouldn't it just come in and do its stuff? Because the power of God is never forced upon anyone. God comes to you by invitation only. Ever is He there...He/She there. Ever is the power ready. Ever is the love available, always, ever, ever with *no* exception. But it has to be invited in. There has to be something in the soul of you that says, "Come in. I welcome You. I want to know You are here. I want to be at one with You," and instantly when that thought is thought, instantly that healing power rushes in.

Everybody thinks that healing...if a healing is to be successful, the person lives on and their physical body is sound and well. Some people use the healing power to pass away with. If they are fearful, terribly, terribly fearful of death and they haven't the courage quite to go, they will take that healing power and they will use it to heal themselves of the fear of death and then they will let go and pass over.

How many of you here are afraid to die? Every single one of you is. Consciously, a lot of you say, "No, I'm not afraid to die," but if a knock came upon your door and you opened the door and the Angel of Death stood there and says, "Hi, I'm here for your baggage," I can guarantee that every single one of you would say, "Well, could you just give me five minutes?" (Laughter)

Participant: Is there an Angel of Death for real?

Gabriel: Well, there's probably about several million of them. There's not a single...I mean, we're good but... (Laughter) Yes, there are angels of death. Now an angel of death—don't be misled—can't take you if you're not ready to go. An angel of death can't come in and say, "Okay kid, I got three seconds. Come on. We're out of here." (Laughter) It doesn't work like that. The Angel of Death comes and waits, and when you surrender, the Angel of Death very lovingly, very sweetly takes you to loved ones, to light, to joy, and to love and peace.

Do they look like great specters with skull faces? No, they are actually quite beautiful, quite beautiful, filled with light, absolutely unconditional love, and sweet gentleness. They're nothing to be afraid of by any means. I've met a lot in my day. I've found them rather pleasant. Not too talkative but rather pleasant.

I suppose when all you do is deal with dead people you don't have much to say! (Laughter)

When a person uses the healing power to pass into spirit, as you call it, that healing power goes with them and remains with them as long as they need it. Now you might think, "Well, why would anyone in the spirit world need healing?" Because a lot of people hold onto their old concepts, old error perceptions, old religious beliefs, old hurts, old wounds, old thoughts of revenge, old feelings of hatred, and so forth. And the healing power is used in the spirit world to heal them of those error perceptions and of those misguided thoughts.

What happens to a person who appears not to have any reason to want to leave the earth and they suddenly have a crash and in the crash they are taken into spirit? I've told you before... They have planned that way back up here in the soul. They have planned that on such and such a day of earth time they will leave the earth very quickly. Remember, you all plan how you leave, when you leave, where you leave, and whether or not with whom you will leave.

Some people prefer to leave in groups. That's why you have aeroship crashes and so forth. It is because people choose to leave in a group. Safety in numbers or something, I don't know. (Laughter) But anyone who chooses to leave...when family friends and so forth send them light and love, it travels with them and heals them of any misperceived concepts that they have.

Now, there are 740 some different religions upon your earth. All of them wrong, but that's beside the point. (Laughter) They all have a silver thread of truth in them but basically, every single one of them is way off the wall. So you have 740 some different ways of praying and every single method is effective, every single method. But every single method of prayer and belief system has its own vibratory rate and it works toward healing within that vibratory rate.

It doesn't work the same. For example, prayer of healing from the Hebrew people is different from that of a Catholic, the Catholic is different from that of the Presbyterian, the Baptists, the Methodists, the Born-Once-Mores...they all present a different vibratory rate in their way of praying. Are their prayers all heard? Absolutely.

But let us be real here. Now, ninety-nine and forty-four percent of all prayer for the well-being of another person is generated by fear—fear of harm coming to them, fear that they're going to die, fear that they're not going to be well, fear that something's going to happen to them, fear that the person doing the praying will never see them again, and so forth. So, ninety-nine percent of prayer is based on fear.

What do you think is going to happen when you pray from fear? What kind of a prayer power do you think you're going to get? A very negative one, indeed, and what you're going to get out of that is such a mixture. Instead of the pure, direct line which comes from the prayer of trust, you're going to get a garbled, sharp-edged, blotched up vibratory rate that's going to go directly to the person you're praying for. And is it going to surround them with love and light and glory? Oh, no, no, no, no. It's going to surround them with the heebie-jeebies! (Laughter) Because they're not going to be feeling all the love and power that there is in prayer. They're going to be feeling the fear, the jolts, the stabs, all of that kind of thing.

It comes like spurts of electrical shock into their aura, into the surrounding area of their aura, and it remains like that as long as fear is involved. It remains like that. If you want to feel absolute prayerful fear, go into the place in your hospitals where you keep the babies that are born too soon. There you have the love and the longing of the parents mixed with *unmitigated fear*. So you have this prayer power that's shot full of like electrical shocks and this is what surrounds the little soul coming in.

Now if the parents, especially I should say the mother, can go and see that child with absolute trust that whatever that little soul has chosen is going to be carried forth with love and with perfection, and release that child to its highest good, whatever that good may be, without fear, the power of that healing that goes around that child almost always, with very few exceptions, gives the child strength and the impetus to remain.

But when the little ones feel only the fear and the stabbing sharpness of fear that fear produces, they don't want to stay because it's not a comforting, comfortable place to be. It's a very uncomfortable place to be and a lot of times they seek to get away from it, which means that they will leave the physical body.

Just about all of the religions, with the exceptions of a few here and there, are taught to pray out of fear. Tinkerbell is afraid I'm going to open my mouth and put Beloved Woman's both feet in it. (Laughter)

I cannot say that there is one religion that is worse than the others. They're all pretty bad. When it comes to teaching you to be afraid of God... Because you are taught from the time you're little that if you do something you shouldn't, God's going to get you. Some of them even teach you if you are sick, you're being punished, and if there's something wrong with you, well then, most assuredly, you are the sinner of sinners.

So, when you approach God with the idea that He's going to get you, do you think you're going to draw to you divine love? You would push it away. You would block it out. And when you are so guilt-ridden and you really believe that you have done something that is so unforgivable, that it can never be reconciled in any way or form...

When you pray, you don't expect to get results, even though you say, "I'll ask God and God will take care of it." What you're really saying is, "I'll ask God but He isn't going to care. He's not going to do anything. How could He do anything for me when I am so wretched indeed?"

So what happens? Now you have the power of prayer coming swirling in and you've got a wall here of guilt. The power of prayer comes in and it meets this wall of guilt. Now, it's going to wrap around that guilt just as the healing power wraps around the aura. It's going to wrap around that guilt and it is going to abide there. It's going to sit there and it's going to wait until such time as the guilt begins to loosen. And when the guilt begins to loosen, then the power begins to come in.

Now, how many of you here think you aren't feeling subconsciously guilty for something? You know you are, indeed. Now, guilt is a strange thing. You know what guilt looks like? It looks like rock, gray rock. Some of it is darker than others but it looks like rock and it forms sheets of itself, something like one after the other and one after the other, and the longer you hold that guilt, the more solid it becomes until finally it's really like rock.

If you have held it for, say 2,000 years for example, then you've got a wall about as thick as this room is wide of solid rock. Now that is going to certainly prevent any healing power from reaching into you, isn't it? It's not going to let it in because you're standing inside here and you're saying, "I don't deserve to be healed. I don't deserve to be helped. I don't deserve anything. So please pray for me and I'll sit here and not take it in."

Now this is not a conscious thing. Most people don't consciously do this but when you have been prayed for by even one person and you aren't getting any better, guess what you've got? Rock.

So, how does one deal with that? After all, one is on the inside of this rock. Here's the person and here's the rock. The only way to break away the rock is from within. No one else can break it away from the outside. The power of prayer will wait around it just as the healing power waits around the aura. It will wait around that wall. If it takes another 2,000 years, it will wait around that wall.

So, the work has to be internal. You can have saints praying for you. You can have the Master Jesus himself come down. And unless you're willing to tear down the guilt from within you, none of that's going to do any good.

How do you tear it down from within? We're going to get into that.

When you pray from faith, from trust... How many of you here feel that you absolutely, one hundred percent, trust God? Are you holding her hand or is she holding yours up? (Laughter) One of you does and the other one doesn't so, "Get your hand up!" Is that it? (Laughter)

If you trust God completely to the extent whereby you feel that nothing that God offers you can ever be anything but good, even if you don't like the wrappings that it comes in, do you trust that within the package there is a blessing? "Not all the time," is correct, indeed. Because if you absolutely felt that way all the time, you wouldn't have any fear...of anything. When a friend was ill, you wouldn't feel that they might not remain on the earth. When your finances were in jeopardy, you wouldn't feel that you are going to end up in the pauper's house. When there was a disagreement between you and your mate, you wouldn't feel that your marriage was on the sand or rocks or whatever. You wouldn't fear anything because you would know, "This has come to bless me."

But most people go through a time of abject *terror* when something happens. It's, "Oh dear, oh dear!" It takes you sometimes anywhere from a half an hour to two or three hours or sometimes a week before you settle down and you think, "Oh, I forgot. Yes. This has come to bless me. Oh God, I wish it would!" (Laughter)

But the real *belief* that it has come to bless you is not real to you. You may affirm it. You may say, "This has come to bless me. Oh, please let me know that it has *really* come to bless me. I know it has come to bless me. Yes, it has. What if? I never thought of that before. Oh, no. I'm not going to do that. This has come to bless me. I wish I were dead!" (Laughter) Now we go through that, don't you? So, you cannot sit there and say, "I absolutely trust God," because if you did, you wouldn't go through that.

Now, you asked, "How do you break down these walls of granite that have been created by guilt?" You throw out all your religious beliefs. [To Tinkerbell] No, the Pope's not going to get me! (Laughter) They haven't in all these years.

Now, I don't care what religious background you come from. They have all taught you fear. And I'm not telling you not to go to your churches or your synagogues. I'm just telling you, don't believe in fear. God is not going to get you.

So, how does one get rid of a lifetime of programming in which you are taught that anything bad that happens to you is God punishing you for some perceived evil doing? You start, first of all, by talking to God. I don't mean formal prayer. I don't mean reciting your beads or reading from a book. I mean sitting down and saying,

> Father, here I am and I'm scared. Such and such a thing has happened to me and right now, at this moment, I am so afraid. I know that You know the outcome, but I

don't. I don't want to be afraid. I want to trust You. I want to believe that this truly has come to bless me but at this moment, I'm not in that space. But You can make me be there. You can surround me with Your love in such a way that I can feel it, and as I feel it, I will know You are truly here loving me and if You love me, then I don't have anything to be afraid of. I know if I feel Your love, that I can trust that You will not lead me into the valley of shadows but You will establish my feet upon the firmament of Your substance. And when my feet are thusly established, I can lift my eyes and look at You and know how much You love me. Help me to know how much You love me.

A simple prayer like that opens the door between you and God. God never closes His door but you close yours. You close it in fear, in guilt, in shame, and in a thousand things.

And getting yourself reconnected to that established knowing that you once had—that you were created with, that you and God are one—that helps you to see yourself as someone loved by God because until you believe that God loves you, you're not going to believe that only good comes to you. You're not going to be able to believe, "This has come to bless me," because you're still going to have your walls of guilt.

Now, God loves you. Whether you know it or not, God loves you. But when you know God loves you, it helps you to talk to God about why you feel guilty. It helps you to say, "Father, I perceive that I have done thus-and-so and I know now that it was not a correct thing for me to do and I'm very sorry that I did it but the fact remains I did it and I can't undo it but I can accept that I am forgiven. I can accept that You love me and You hold nothing against me. I can accept Your peace. I can know that You love me."

Now you might have to say that a hundred times a day but you begin and you say it and you feel it. You feel it and as you do, those walls come down. They crumble. Holes come in them 'til after a bit, they fall completely away and you are free.

Now you have to understand that most people very rarely do anything so-called bad on purpose, and most of you realize your so-called mistakes only in retrospect, only as you think back on it, but at the moment it's going on, it seems all right at the moment, doesn't it? And only afterwards you think, "Uh, I never should have done that."

If you hold to guilt, then you are not forgiving yourself and if you don't forgive yourself, then you can't forgive someone else. You cannot reach out in forgiveness to another until you forgive yourself, until you say, "I'm all right. I didn't mean any harm and I'm really, really all right."

And talk to God every day about how you feel. You know, people think they only can say certain words to God. They can get up in the morning and be in an absolutely foul mood and go off to church and go in there and kneel down and say, "[Inaudible] I'm here and I pray that You give me a good day. Goodbye. See You tomorrow," and out the door they go. (Laughter)

The thing is, when you rise in the morning, if you are in a foul mood, you say, "Dear God, I am in a terrible mood. I don't like being in this mood. I want to be in a peaceful mood. Please grant me a peaceful mood." Then you can talk to God as you go on your way to work. You can say, "Look at that idiot ahead of us, God. (Laughter) Would You please bless them out of my way. (Laughter) Thank you, Father, I'm grateful for Your help."

It's entirely possible to have a running conversation with God all day long. You can talk to Him about anything, anything at all and as you do, what do you think is happening? You are establishing a *contact with God that is solid and very real.* Then you can start talking to Him about all the things that bothered you that you didn't know bothered you because these thoughts will present themselves for your contemplation.

And you can think about them and you could say, "Father, you know, I hadn't thought about this in a long time but this thought came into my mind and, you know, I really think I would like to change my thinking about that. Show me a good way to think about that," and then accept it. Accept it.

Tinker says I should tell a little story about Beloved Woman. [To Tinkerbell] I wasn't there. What did she do? Oh, all right.

She went to get her food supplies in and it was very cold and she hadn't dressed warmly enough so she was in a bit of a hurry, and as she went to take them out of her transport thing there, the bags broke and everything went all over the ground and being on a little incline, some of the stuff rolled away. (Laughter)

I can remember a time she would have fumed all over the place about that but instead she said, "Well, Father, look what we've done! (Laughter) You wait here and watch the stuff. I'll go get another bag." (Laughter) And that's exactly what she did. She went in and she brought forth from her abode a bag and she gathered up the stuff and she thanked God for keeping it safe in her absence. And then she carried it forth into the house.

You can hold conversations with God about anything. The other morn, she got up and said to God, "Well, what shall we have for breakfast?" (Laughter) And then after making her selection, she thanked Him and said, "That was a good suggestion. I'm glad You thought of that."

Engage God in conversation. Bring that awareness into your life in your everyday things. It's called "practicing the Presence," and there is *nothing* that gets rid of guilt or sorrow or anything or breaks down the barriers of the walls of guilt faster than engaging God in every part of your life. Now, you don't have to talk out loud to Him if you're in a group. You can talk in your mind.

Beloved Woman took a friend of hers out to dine and as they walked in—the place was rather crowded...Tinker's telling me this—and as she stepped in the door and looked around, she said, "Oh Lord, where shall we sit?" [Gabriel laughs] I don't think *he* was there but anyway, God was. And straight away someone got up and left the table and then there they had a place to sit and she said, "Thank you, Lord."

Now, the point is that anything, anything, anything that connects you to your God-self, to that awareness of the presence of God with you, always, ever, is the only way that you're going to break away the walls of guilt, even though they be 2,000 years old, or break away anger, break away feelings of unforgiveness, break away anything that keeps you from that At-one-ment with God. Hold conversations with Him about everything from what you're going to wear that day to anything on earth that you want to talk about. It's a wonderful practice.

Have you anything to ask of me?

Participant: This conversation with God then. Even though we...all this soul stuff that's going on, we don't have a conscious idea of it.

Gabriel: No, you don't.

Participant: So this conversation with God will help balance everything?

Gabriel: Yes, because what it does, beloved woman, it opens the channels that you have closed between you and the awareness of God's presence in your life. And when you do that, it purges you. It brings up issues that you can look at quite objectively without your emotions getting in and you can clear away a lot of debris that you have accumulated.

Participant: So in doing this, we're breaking down the barriers so that this healing that everyone's been sending us can flow in.

Gabriel: Absolutely, it can come in because you don't have any resistance to it.

Participant: And even though some of us may already have a resistance ourselves that we're not consciously aware of, this will break that away?

Gabriel: Indeed, it will because what you're doing, beloved woman, you are bringing in the power of your own God-self, of your connectedness to God, and when you do that, it breaks down every barrier. Perfect love casts out fear and that's what this is doing, connecting you to that perfect love.

Participant: So it's building trust.

Gabriel: Building trust, indeed.

Participant: I have a question around the soul. When we have conversations with God and we have daily conversations with God and we are breaking away that barrier, that wall, does that disappear some of the memories of our soul?

Gabriel: Oh, indeed. Whenever you willingly release something, what you perceive to be a past mistake or whatever that would cause you guilt and so forth, whenever that happens, it just is *blinked* right out of the soul memory. It's just gone.

Participant: It's gone. And that also goes for an illness in your physical body that may have come from a past life?

Gabriel: Yes.

Particpant: Okay, great. Thank you.

Gabriel: Well, that's the other thing perhaps I should address. Illness is brought about in this life, manifesting in this life, that have started in another lifetime. A lot of times your thought process from what you perceive to be a previous lifetime will have seed effects. In other words, there will be seeds sown in

179

your subconscious mind that would bring you into the manifestation of an illness. Now you can change that at any point. All you have to do is change your mind. "I do not want this illness. I do not want to manifest any kind of negativity."

The other thing is, your past...you are a result now, today in your time, of what you have been, the collective ideas of what you have lived in other lifetimes. In other words, your belief system, not who you were or what type of work you did, but your belief system from other lifetimes makes you what you are this day in time, and this lifetime will make you what you would be in your next and so on and so forth. So if you want to get rid of the garbage, so to speak, you will be changing all the future lifetimes that you have by getting rid of all the gook now.

Participant: I have a question about time. I know it's an illusion but the time...I'm looking at how illnesses get manifested in your body at very young ages.

Gabriel: That is usually from a past life, karmic.

Participant: It comes from a past life, so all right. Even at that young age?

Gabriel: Oh yes, because the soul has the memory. The body only obeys what is told to it.

Participant: I think I have been a little bit confused on how and on what subject matter we address God. Somewhere along in my learning, I had felt that directly God was responsible and helping us with our spiritual growth, not our daily, every day, minute things, and that for the daily things, we were to talk more with—some people would say their guides, other people would say their Masters, others would say angels—that these are all beings who are from God who are of spirit who are here to help us on earth, and these are the beings that would deal with the mundane, the everyday kind of things. And I get very confused as to whom I wanted to address, whom I wanted to call in, and be with. And my direct ...

Gabriel: Anybody you want to. Beloved woman, first of all, do not remove God so from you. When you cannot talk to God about the daily things, then you are saying, "I cannot approach the throne of God excepting on a certain day or a certain time or for a certain reason." Talk to God about everything. You can talk to... Beloved Woman holds conversations with angels, with guides, with her grandmother, with God, whoever—talks to the cat, you know, whatever (laughter)—but the point is that you can talk to anyone about anything. Whatever feels comfortable for you at the time.

Participant: Because I like to go to the top and why would I ... (Laughter)

Gabriel: And why *wouldn't* you go to the top? Why would you feel you couldn't approach God about the daily things? You are *in* the daily things.

Participant: Right, and obviously God is part of my higher self so that it's all one anyway.

Gabriel: Absolutely.

Participant: Good, I feel much better because I would rather just talk with God about these smaller matters in life and let truth flow into me.

Gabriel: Talk to God about anything and everything. And Tinker says, "That's good!" She's happy. It gets her off the hook. (Laughter)

Participant: A few days ago I had to make an emergency flight and I had to carry my baggage. I was by myself. And getting into the airport I was saying, "Oh, boy. How is this going to..." I didn't want to bother anybody so I assume I was asking for help and as I walked in, there's a basket, like a pushcart, just like that, standing there. I look at it and I go, "Thank you, my Lord. Thank you." And right away I put my baggage on there because there it was and that was through the whole time I had this experience.

Gabriel: You were taken care of as you ever are.

Participant: I was taken care of. It was beautiful.

Participant: When a person builds up the guilt and prayers are offered for that person, you said that they stay outside in the aura.

Gabriel: Outside of the aura, yes.

Participant: Then does it not do any good to pray for that person?

Gabriel: Oh, no, no, no. Not at all. It certainly does good because it collects around the aura and as the person is ready and willing to allow it in, it penetrates and comes in. So absolutely pray for others. Yes, indeed.

Participant: But if they don't let it in for a couple of lifetimes or something?

Gabriel: It still does them good.

Participant: In their present lifetime, it still does them good?

Gabriel: As much as they will allow, yes. But even if it is several lifetimes hence before they take it in, it still is a blessing to them at that time.

Participant: Okay.

Gabriel: Haven't you ever met people who seem to live charmed lives?

Participant: Yes.

Gabriel: How do you think they got there? It is when they begin to allow the prayers that have accumulated over the centuries, sometimes for many hundreds of years, all of a sudden it's like a light goes on and, "Oh, I can...I can take this in," and all of the blessings start manifesting their lives and they manifest that way from all of the prayers that have ever been said for them.

Participant: That was my next question. They get some of this work done, then all of these blessings or prayers pour in upon them. That's how if manifests then?

Gabriel: Yes.

Participant: Okay. Sometimes I feel like our prayers are just floating around and not attaching themselves where we want them to go, but they're there.

Gabriel: They are absolutely there. I promise you that.

Participant: Okay, thank you.

Participant: So we all probably have a lot of untapped prayers and healing energy around us at this very moment. I have in my aura a lot of things, probably, that I could take advantage of.

Gabriel: Absolutely you do. Absolutely.

Participant: So we could just let that in?

Gabriel: You can let it in any time.

Participant: My question is in regards to the premature babies, the newborn babies. Do babies, the newborn babies that are born in the earth that are premature, have a prayer of fear or a prayer of trust in their existence?

Gabriel: From them, you mean? Concerning themselves?

Participant: Yes, more so than the parents.

Gabriel: It is usually a prayer of trust. For one thing, remember, they have planned to come as a premature baby. There is a reason for that, a reason for them and a reason for the parents involved. So, their action is always in trust. It is from the parents that you get the fear.

Participant: And because these babies have just arrived coming from our heavenly Father and they have not experienced life...

Gabriel: Oooh...

Participant: Well, excuse me, I take that back. I understand. On a new realm.

Gabriel: Indeed, they have. They have had many previous lifetimes upon the earth.

Participant: I slipped there. I understand. I thank you. (Laughter) I've answered my own question, I think.

Gabriel: Yes, you have.

Participant: I'm curious about guilt that you say is 2,000 years old. Is that specific that it's ...?

Gabriel: I just grabbed a time out of the air.

Participant: Does the origin of our guilt matter?

Gabriel: No, not at all. The thing is it doesn't matter where it came from or why you have it. It matters only that you get rid of it.

Participant: Such a comforting lesson of self-improvement and prayer and our relationship to our heavenly Father. My question is as follows: in regards to the Angel of Death, this question is not being asked in a direction coming from fear. When our soul makes that final decision to leave this earth plane, do we have a choice to be greeted by people that we knew and loved in this earth plane first?

Gabriel: Absolutely. Most people don't even see the Angel of Death. It's an unseen presence that assists in that little split second when you step out of the body and the silver cord is severed. There is that abiding, loving presence there, which is the Angel of Death. Most people don't even turn around to look but if they did, they would not be afraid. And yes, you are greeted ever by loved ones who have preceded you.

Participant: I have a question regarding the death process. I'm wondering if there can be a moment of confusion for some people when they pass over where they get stuck...the so-called ghosts that we speak of.

Gabriel: Oh well, some people are very attached to the earth plane and they don't want to leave it, or they may be attached to a particular home, a particular object, a particular room.

Participant: Is there a way that we, being in this realm, can help them move on or is it our duty, our obligation, or whatever?

Gabriel: Well, it 'tis is not an obligation by any means. It 'tis a loving act to pray them into the light, to always say to them, "Go to the light," and envision the light near to them and so forth. But until they are ready to go, they aren't going to budge. Angels come and they try to bring them up and some of them will go a little ways and then they go back and others will say, "Oh, I can get out of here? Fine," and they go on. It depends upon how strongly they are attached to whatever it is they are attached to.

Participant: I have a question about varied spiritual beliefs or backgrounds. I have done a lot of reading in various areas. I have a book of Tarot and some cards and different bookstores offer tarot readings and they look harmless. They look...pretty pictures, and it's hard to understand what they mean. And I wonder if you could comment on how this comes into play.

Gabriel: It is merely a point of concentration, that's all. The person doing the reading is very psychic but they believe they need something to use and so they use the Tarot or tea leaves or whatever.

Participant: Okay. So it's not a harmful background?

Gabriel: No.

Participant: But the pictures...there are stars, there are crosses piercing the heart, there are swords, there's nines, nine stars...

Gabriel: But those are all symbols of things that are not physical. They are symbolic of thought processes. Like anything else, the Tarot is merely a tool to use and nothing more. Those are all symbolisms, and that, like anything else, is merely a tool and nothing more, just a tool to use.

Participant: I came across a book about Paul Twitchell, who I've never heard of, and the book is very much about soul work, and he is termed the founder of Eckankar and I wonder if you could comment on what that is.

Gabriel: It is a very misguided rationale that tries to pigeonhole things that he knows little about. A little bit of knowledge taken in the wrong direction, even though the intent be pure, can do a lot of misleading.

Participant: We know that these channeling sessions will be ending soon and you will be leaving us. Will you tell us before you leave so that we can say goodbye?

Gabriel: Oh, absolutely. I should be out of here one year from this month that you are in. Are you in your eleventh month? Then one year from this month I shall be gone.

Participant: I am so grateful to be here at this place and time so that I could be taught by an angel. It has been quite an honor.

Gabriel: Well, thank you, beloved woman.

Well, I have enjoyed being with you all this night and I shall see you again. I'm going to have a prayer with you.

Dear Father of light,
Mother of goodness,
Holy Spirit of peace,
we are thankful for Your presence here in this room.

We are thankful for Your unending love,
for Your wisdom and Your truth.
We thank you that these, Thy children,
gather here this night to learn, to grow, to evolve.

We thank you, Father God,
for the richest blessing of all,
divine love that binds us all to Thee.

And so it is.

Index

Index

Index

Index

Index

Index

About the Author

Reverend Penny Donovan, a natural medium since childhood, was ordained in 1960 at the John Carlson Memorial Institute in Buffalo, NY. She obtained her Doctor of Divinity degree from the Fellowships of the Spirit in Buffalo, NY. In 1964 Rev. Penny founded the Trinity Temple of the Holy Spirit Church in Albany, NY, and served as the pastor there for thirty years. In 1994 she retired from that position to devote full time to spreading the teachings of Archangel Gabriel whom she had channeled from 1987 to 1999. Since Gabriel's departure, Rev. Penny has continued teach and conduct spiritual healing sessions in classes and retreats.

88417130R00122

Made in the USA
Columbia, SC
05 February 2018